# NEED to KNOW

# OCR A-LEVEL GEOGRAPHY

David Redfern

## HODDER
EDUCATION
AN HACHETTE UK COMPANY

Hachette UK's policy is to use papers that are natural, renewable and recyclable products and made from wood grown in sustainable forests. The logging and manufacturing processes are expected to conform to the environmental regulations of the country of origin.

Orders: please contact Bookpoint Ltd, 130 Park Drive, Milton Park, Abingdon, Oxon OX14 4SE. Telephone: (44) 01235 827827. Fax: (44) 01235 400401. Email: education@bookpoint.co.uk

Lines are open from 9 a.m. to 5 p.m., Monday to Saturday, with a 24-hour message answering service. You can also order through our website: www.hoddereducation.co.uk

ISBN: 978 1 5104 2855 3

© David Redfern

First published in 2018 by

Hodder Education,
An Hachette UK Company
Carmelite House
50 Victoria Embankment
London EC4Y 0DZ

Impression number     10 9 8 7 6 5 4 3 2 1

Year      2022 2021 2020 2019 2018

Typeset in India by Aptara Inc.

Printed in Spain

A catalogue record for this title is available from the British Library.

MIX
Paper from
responsible sources
FSC™ C104740

# Contents

# Getting the most from this book

This *Need to Know* guide is designed to help you throughout your course as a companion to your learning and a revision aid in the months or weeks leading up to the final exams.

The following features in each section will help you get the most from the book.

## You need to know
Each topic begins with a list summarising what you 'need to know' in this topic for the exam.

## Exam tip
Key knowledge you need to demonstrate in the exam, tips on exam technique, common misconceptions to avoid and important things to remember.

## Key terms
Definitions of highlighted terms in the text to make sure you know the essential terminology for your subject.

## Do you know?
Questions at the end of each topic to test you on some of its key points. Check your answers here: www.hoddereducation.co.uk/needtoknow/answers

## Synoptic links
Reminders of how knowledge and skills from different topics in your A-level relate to one another.

## End of section questions
Questions at the end of each main section of the book to test your knowledge of the specification area covered. Check your answers here: www.hoddereducation.co.uk/needtoknow/answers

# 1 Coastal landscapes

## 1.1 Coastal systems

### You need to know

- coastal landscapes can be viewed as systems
- how coastal landscape systems are influenced by a range of physical factors
- the main sources of sediment in a coastal system

## Systems

Coastal landscapes act as natural open systems, with inputs, processes and outputs (Table 1).

Table 1 Features of a coastal system

| Inputs | **Marine:** energy from waves; tides and sea currents; salt spray |
| --- | --- |
| | **Geological:** rock type; rock structure; products of weathering |
| | **Atmospheric:** wind energy; precipitation; temperature; sea level change |
| | **Human activity:** land use; coastal protection |
| Weathering/erosional processes | **Weathering:** physical; chemical; biological |
| | **Erosion:** hydraulic action; wave quarrying; abrasion; attrition |
| | **Mass movement:** landslides; rockfalls; mudflows; rotational slips; soil creep |
| Erosional components | **Erosional landforms and landscapes:** cliffs; headlands and bays; wave-cut platforms; geos; caves, arches and stacks |
| Transport processes (flows) | **Water transport:** longshore drift; onshore and offshore movement; traction; saltation; suspension |
| | **Wind transport:** surface creep; saltation |
| Depositional components (stores) | **Depositional landforms and landscapes:** beaches; spits; tombolos; bars and barrier beaches; sand dunes; salt marshes |
| Outputs | Energy; onshore sediment; marine sediment |

## Feedback

Energy and material flow (transfer) through the coastal system, often involving feedback mechanisms.

An example of positive feedback:
- sea walls prevent flooding, but they also limit cliff erosion
- this restricts the release of sediment into the coastal system

- this sediment might otherwise have been re-deposited and helped protect the coastline

An example of negative feedback:

- sediment is eroded from a beach during a storm, and is then deposited offshore to form a bar
- waves break before reaching the beach, dissipating their energy and therefore reducing erosion of the beach
- normal wave conditions re-work offshore deposits back to the beach

## Sediment cells and budgets

Sediment cells:

- DEFRA has identified eleven major sediment cells for England and Wales, which form the basic units for coastal management
- each cell is separated by headlands or stretches of open water
- most cells are divided into sub-cells
- sediment cell theory is a key component of Shoreline Management Plans, which decide on future strategies of coastal management (see page 19)

Sediment budgets:

- see Figure 1

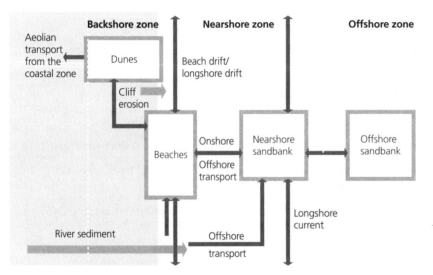

Figure 1 Coastal sediment budgets

# Physical factors
## Wind and waves

Key points:

- waves are caused by the wind blowing over the surface of the sea
- as wind drags over the water surface, friction causes a disturbance and forms waves
- waves at sea follow an orbital movement — objects on the water do not travel forward

---

**Key terms**

**Negative feedback** Acts to lessen the effect of the original change and ultimately to reverse it.

**Sediment (or littoral) cell** A length of coastline and its associated near-shore area, within which the movement of coarse sediment (sand and shingle) is largely self-contained.

**DEFRA** The Department for Environment, Food and Rural Affairs.

**Exam tip**

The UK case study of a coastal landscape in Section 1.2 Coastal landforms (page 15) will require you to know which DEFRA cell, or sub-cell, it is located in.

**Key term**

**Sediment budget** The relationship between accretion and erosion, which can be used to predict the changing shape of a coastline over time.

- when a wave reaches shallow water, the movement of the base of the wave is slowed by friction with the sea bed
- the wave spills forward as a breaker, moving objects forward with it in the swash
- it then draws back to the sea as backwash

Wave energy is controlled by:
- the force of the wind and its direction
- the duration of the wind
- the fetch — the longer the fetch, the more energy waves possess

There are three types of breaking wave:
- spilling — waves breaking on to gently sloping beaches; water flows gently forward as the wave breaks
- plunging — steep waves breaking on to steep beaches; water falls vertically downwards
- surging — low-angle waves breaking on to steep beaches; the wave slides forward

Constructive waves:
- build beaches
- are the product of distant weather systems
- have longer wavelengths, lower height and are less frequent (6–8 per minute)
- swash is greater than backwash so they add to beach materials, giving rise to a gently sloping beach
- the upper part of such a beach is marked by a series of small ridges called berms (see Figure 4 on page 14)

Destructive waves:
- have a shorter wavelength, a greater height and are more frequent (10–14 per minute)
- backwash is greater than the swash so that sediment is dragged offshore
- create a steeper beach profile initially, though over time the beach will flatten as material is drawn backwards
- form shingle ridges at the back of a beach (storm beaches — Figure 4), created by local storms

## Tides

Key points:
- tides are produced by the gravitational pull of the moon and the sun — as the moon orbits the Earth, high tides follow it

> ### Key terms
>
> **Swash** The landward flow of water up a beach.
>
> **Backwash** The seaward flow of water down a beach.
>
> **Fetch** The distance over which the wind has blown to produce waves.
>
> **Berm** A small ridge at the back of a beach, corresponding to a previous high tide.
>
> **Tides** The periodic rise and fall in the level of the water in the oceans caused by the gravitational attraction of the moon and sun.

> ### Exam tip
>
> When asked to compare or contrast different types of waves, make sure you make clear comparative statements rather than separate statements.

- the moon pulls water towards it and there is a compensatory bulge on the opposite side of the Earth
- at various locations between the two bulges, there is a low tide
- the highest tides occur when the moon and sun are aligned, when the gravitational pull is at its strongest
- this happens twice each lunar month and results in spring tides with a high tidal range
- twice a month, the moon and the sun are at right angles to each other and the gravitational pull is therefore at its weakest, producing neap tides with a low range

Tidal ranges:
- are low in enclosed seas — wave action is restricted to a narrow area of land
- are higher in places where the coast is funnelled, such as estuaries

## Geology

Key points:
- some rock types (e.g. clay) have a weak lithology, with little resistance to erosion, weathering and mass movements
- others (e.g. basalt, granite) are made of dense interlocking crystals and are very resistant
- porous rocks (e.g. chalk) have a structure with tiny air spaces that separate the mineral particles, allowing them to absorb and store water
- carboniferous limestone is also permeable because of its many joints

## Ocean currents

Key points (Figure 2):
- warm ocean currents transfer heat-energy from low latitudes towards the poles
- cold ocean currents move cold water from polar regions towards the Equator
- an ocean current has limited impact on coastal landscape processes
- the transfer of heat-energy can be significant — it directly affects air temperature and therefore the sub-aerial processes of weathering and mass movement (see pages 10–11)

**Exam tip**

Note that tides only reinforce the action of waves; tidal range is the main factor in coastal processes.

**Key terms**

Tidal range  The difference between the water level at high tide and at low tide.

Lithology  The physical and chemical composition of rocks.

Structure  The properties of individual rock types, such as jointing, bedding and faulting, which affect the permeability of rocks.

Ocean currents  Flows of water generated by the Earth's rotation, set in motion by the movement of winds across the water surface.

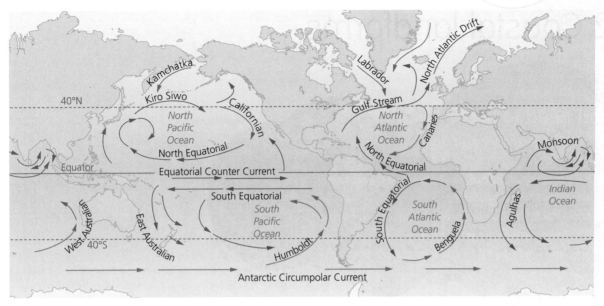

**Figure 2 Ocean currents**

# Sediment sources

The various sources of sediment:

- rivers — material is weathered and eroded inland and deposited in their mouths/estuaries or taken out to sea
- the sea bed — brought from offshore deposits by waves in storms
- erosion of the coastline — especially from weak cliffs made of soft rock
- transported material — blown by wind (aeolian) or moved along a coast (longshore drift)
- human activity — through **beach nourishment**

> ### Key term
>
> **Beach nourishment** The addition of sand or pebbles to an existing beach to make it higher or wider.

> ### Do you know?
>
> 1 Referring to one coastal area you have studied, identify the main stores in that area.
> 2 Identify one feedback mechanism arising from human activity in a coastal area.
> 3 What causes a wave to break?
> 4 Explain why a plan view of an area may be useful when describing the effects of geology on a coastline.

# 1.2 Coastal landforms

## You need to know

- the main geomorphological processes that act on a coastline
- how coastal landforms can be created by erosional and depositional processes
- how coastal landscapes are made up of a variety of landforms, which are inter-related
- how and why coastal landscapes change over time

## Processes

### Physical weathering

Frost shattering:

- takes place in rocks that contain crevices and joints, and where temperatures fluctuate around 0°C
- water enters the joints and, during cold nights, freezes
- as ice occupies around 9% more volume than water, it exerts pressure within the joint
- this alternating freeze–thaw process slowly widens the joints, eventually causing bits to break off from the main body of rock
- leads to the formation of scree slopes

Salt weathering:

- takes place when a rock becomes saturated with water that contains salt
- some of the salt crystallises and begins to exert pressure on the rock because the salt crystals are larger than the spaces in which they are being formed
- the process repeats over time and causes the disintegration of the rock

### Chemical weathering

Main features:

- involves the decay or decomposition of rock in situ
- usually takes place in the presence of water, which acts as a dilute acid
- the end products are either soluble and removed in solution, or have a different volume, usually bigger, than the mineral they replace

### Key terms

**Scree** Collections of loose rock at the base of a slope.

**Weathering** Involves the breakdown of rocks into smaller fragments through mechanical processes such as expansion and contraction, mainly due to temperature change.

- the rate tends to increase with rising temperature and humidity levels
- for carbonic acid (carbonation) on limestones, lower temperatures produce greater rates of weathering
- can also occur from the action of dilute acids, resulting both from atmospheric pollution (sulphuric acid) and from the decay of plants and animals (organic acids)

## Mass movement

The rate of **mass movement** (Table 2) depends on:
- the degree of cohesion of the weathered material (**regolith**)
- the steepness of the slope down which the movement takes place
- the amount of water contained in the material

Note: A large amount of water adds weight to the mass, but more importantly lubricates the plane along which movement can take place.

> **Exam tip**
>
> Ensure you know the difference between weathering and erosion processes.

> **Key terms**
>
> **Mass movement** The down-slope movement of weathered material under the influence of gravity.
>
> **Regolith** The collective name for all of the material produced by weathering.

Table 2 Types of mass movement on coasts

| Mass movement | Commentary |
|---|---|
| Creep | - slow downhill movement of soil<br>- tends to operate on slopes steeper than 6°<br>- evidence is shown by small terracettes on a hillside |
| Earthflows | - when regolith becomes saturated, internal friction between the particles is reduced and the debris moves under gravity<br>- can occur on slopes as gentle as 5° once mobile<br>- usually needs a slope of about 10° to initiate movement |
| Mudflows | - occur in areas that experience torrential rain falling on ground that has limited protection from vegetation cover<br>- regolith becomes saturated, increasing the pore pressure in the debris and reducing the frictional resistance between particles<br>- more rapid than earthflows |
| Rock falls | - where erosion is concentrated at the base of a cliff, it becomes unstable and collapses into the sea |
| Landslides | - occur when rocks and/or regolith have bedding planes or when material in one plane/layer becomes very wet and over-lubricated<br>- the added weight from water causes the plane/layer to slip down-slope under gravity over the underlying layers |
| Slumping | - saturated material moves suddenly, resulting in whole sections of cliffs moving down towards a beach<br>- often happens where softer material overlies strata that are far more resistant<br>- the slip plane is often concave, producing a rotational movement |

## Wave erosion

Wave erosion operates by a variety of processes (Table 3).

Table 3 Wave erosion processes

| Erosion process | Commentary |
| --- | --- |
| Hydraulic action | ■ where a wave breaking against rocks traps air into cracks in the rock under pressure, which is then released suddenly as the wave retreats<br>■ causes stress in the rock that creates more cracks, allowing the rock to break up more easily<br>■ also includes pounding — the sheer weight and force of water pushing against a cliff face causing it to weaken |
| Abrasion (corrasion) | ■ where material carried by waves (the load) is used as ammunition to wear away rocks on a cliff or a wave-cut platform as the material is thrown or rubbed against it repeatedly by each wave<br>■ where abrasion is targeted at specific areas such as notches or caves, it is referred to as quarrying |
| Attrition | ■ loose rocks are broken down into smaller and more rounded pebbles, which are then used in abrasion |
| Cavitation | ■ when air bubbles trapped in fast-moving water collapse, causing shock waves to break against the rocks under the water<br>■ repeated shocks of this nature weaken the rock |

## Transportation

Material is transported along a coastline by:

- swash and backwash (see page 7)
- longshore (littoral) drift: material is moved along a shoreline by waves that approach at an angle; swash moves sand and shingle up the beach at an angle but the backwash is at right angles to the beach; this results in material zigzagging its way along the beach according to the prevailing wave direction; material in both suspension and larger fragments is moved this way
- traction: when large stones and pebbles are rolled along the sea bed and across a beach

Material is also eroded and transported in coastal areas by runoff (fluvial erosion) — the flow of water overland either in small channels (rills) or as streams and rivers.

## Deposition

Deposition occurs in low-energy environments, such as bays and estuaries:

- when sand is deposited on a beach and dries out, it can be blown further inland by the wind (aeolian erosion) to form sand dunes at the back of the beach
- in a river estuary, mud and silt can build up in sheltered water to create a salt marsh (see Figure 5 on page 15); here the fresh water of the river meets the salt water of the sea, causing flocculation of suspended material to occur and creating extensive areas of mudflats

### Exam tip

Note, despite what many textbooks state, that solution is *not* a major form of erosion by the sea — the water is too alkaline.

### Key terms

Suspension The process by which very small particles are held in water.

Flocculation The process by which a river's load of clays and silts carried in suspension is deposited more easily on its meeting with sodium chloride in sea water.

# Erosional landforms

Cliffs, headlands and bays:
- form when rocks of differing hardness are exposed together at a coastline
- tougher, more resistant rocks (e.g. granite and limestones) form headlands with cliffs
- weaker rocks (e.g. clays and shales) are eroded to form sandy bays
- **wave refraction** is a key process

Wave-cut (shore) platforms:
- see Figure 3

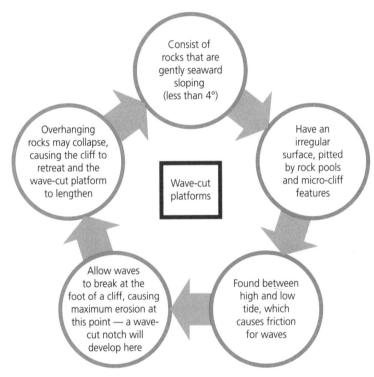

**Figure 3 Wave-cut platforms**

Caves, arches, stacks and stumps:
- erosion takes place on a cliff face where there is a weakness, such as joints or bedding planes
- where waves open up a prolonged joint, they form a deep and steep-sided inlet — a geo
- smaller hollows can be excavated to create caves
- a crack at the rear of a cave may open up like a chimney to the surface of the cliff top — a blow hole
- where caves are created on either side of a headland and are eroded back, they can 'meet' each other (the backwall collapses), forming an arch
- the sea is now able to splash under the arch, further weakening it until eventually the roof collapses leaving the seaward side as a separate island — a stack
- over time the stack erodes to form a stump

# Depositional landforms

Beaches:

- built up by accretion in and across bays — made of sand or shingle, or a mixture of both
- are either swash-aligned — where sediment is taken up and down the beach with little sideways transfer — or drift-aligned, where sediment is transferred along a beach by longshore drift
- can be sub-divided into different zones (see Figure 1 on page 6):
  - ☐ offshore: beyond the influence of breaking waves
  - ☐ nearshore: intertidal and within the breaker zone
  - ☐ backshore: usually above the influence of normal wave patterns, marked at the lower end by berms, and may have a storm beach further up (Figure 4)

> ## Key term
>
> **Accretion** The growth of a natural feature by enlargement. In the case of coasts, sand spits grow by accretion as do other land forms such as sand dunes.

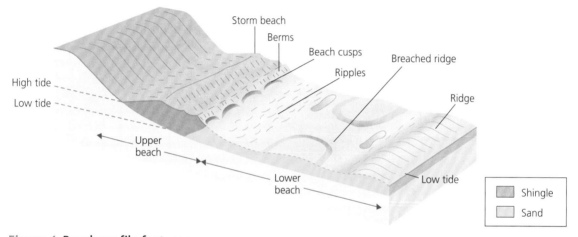

**Figure 4 Beach profile features**

Spits, tombolos:

- are long, narrow stretches of sand/shingle that protrude into the sea or across an estuary
- result from materials being moved along the coast by longshore drift
- this movement continues in the same direction when the coastline curves; where there is an estuary with a strong current that interrupts the movement of material, they project out into it
- the end of the spit is often curved (creating a series of laterals) where waves are refracted around the end of the spit into more sheltered water behind
- a tombolo is where a spit joins the mainland at one end to an island at the other

Onshore bars and barrier beaches:

- a bar is created where a spit has developed right across a bay because there are no strong currents to disturb the process

- this dams brackish water behind it, forming a lagoon
- bars also develop as a result of storms raking up pebbles and, left in ridges offshore, this shingle creates a barrier beach

Salt marshes:

- sheltered river estuaries or the zones in the lee of spits become areas of extensive accumulations of silt and mud (mudflats), aided by flocculation and gentle tides
- these inter-tidal areas are colonised by vegetation, and a succession of plant types may develop over time — a **halosere** — creating a salt marsh (Figure 5)
- the initial plants of a halosere must be tolerant of both salt and regular inundation at high tide — they must also have a long root system and a mat of surface roots to hold the mud in place
- as the mat of vegetation becomes more dense, the impact of the tidal currents reduces; humus levels then increase, allowing reeds and rushes to grow and, later, alder and willow
- salt marshes often have complex systems of waterways — creeks

> ### Key term
>
> **Halosere** The succession of plants that develops in a salt marsh — including eelgrass, spartina grass, cord grass and sea lavender.

> ### Exam tip
>
> A good way to demonstrate you know what each of these erosional and depositional landforms looks like is to draw a sketch. Give it a go!

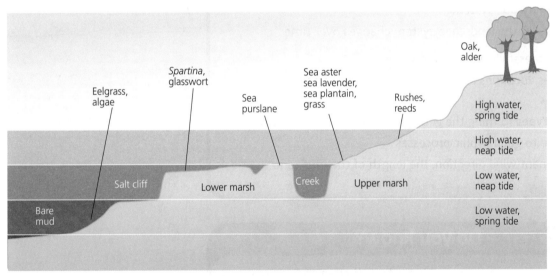

**Figure 5 The structure of a salt marsh**

## Case studies: Coastal landscapes

You are required to study **one high energy coastline** and **one low energy coastline**, at least one of which must be beyond the UK.

High energy coastlines:

- exist where wave power is strong for a greater part of the year
- face the prevailing and dominant wind direction
- face the direction of the longest fetch

Low energy coastlines:

- include estuaries, inlets and sheltered bays
- wave heights are considerably lower than high energy coasts

- waves spread outwards and energy is dissipated, leading to the deposition of transported material

For each of these case studies, you should illustrate:

- physical factors that influence the formation of landforms within the landscape system — geology, winds, tides, waves, sediment cells and sediment sources
- the interrelationship of a range of landforms within the landscape system
- how and why the landscape system changes over time — including short-term changes (e.g. storm events), medium-term changes (e.g. seasonal changes in beach profiles) and long-term changes (e.g. wave-cut platform or spit development)

You should be able to explain:

- how physical factors have influenced geomorphic processes
- how geomorphic processes have led to the development of landforms
- how landforms interrelate with each other
- how and why energy and materials are transferred through the coastal landscape system
- how and why the landscape system changes over time

To do this successfully, you should know:

- the names, locations and approximate scale of a range of landforms
- the rock types forming the geology of the area, and their relative resistance to geomorphic processes
- the dominant wind direction, the length of the fetch and the tidal range

## Exam tips

- Examples of high energy coastlines include Flamborough (Yorkshire), the Jurassic Coast (Dorset), the Land's End Peninsula (Cornwall) and the area near Port Campbell in Australia.
- Examples of low energy coastlines include Morecambe Bay (Lancashire), the Nile Delta (Egypt), the Sundarbans Delta (Bangladesh) and the Baltic Sea.

## Do you know?

1 Give one difference between physical weathering and chemical weathering.
2 What are the key differences between a flow, a slide and a slump?
3 Explain the process of wave refraction.
4 Explain why wave-cut platforms tend to have a maximum width of about 0.5 km.
5 Make two lists: coastal landforms created by erosion, and coastal landforms created by deposition.

# 1.3 Climate change

## You need to know

- the characteristics of emergent coastal landscapes caused by sea level fall
- the characteristics of submergent coastal landscapes caused by sea level rise
- how both of these landscapes will be affected by future climate change

## Emergent coasts

Main points:

- during the early **Pleistocene**, about 100,000 years ago, temperatures were 7°C lower than today
- much water was locked into ice caps and glaciers, and sea levels fell to about 85 m lower than at present
- the effect was to expose land previously covered by the sea, including:
  - ☐ 'abandoned' cliffs: these are no longer being eroded, are isolated from the sea, and have 'fossil' features such as former caves and stacks
  - ☐ raised marine terraces: some are 'stepped', each step representing a standstill in sea level fall
  - ☐ raised beaches: common on the coast of western Scotland, where a series of raised sandy and pebble-strewn areas exist well above the current sea level
- these landforms are no longer affected by wave processes — but they are modified by weathering and mass movement
- as global temperatures rise due to climate change, these landforms:
  - ☐ will become more vegetated and difficult to identify
  - ☐ may be re-submerged as sea levels rise

> ### Key term
>
> **Pleistocene** A geological time period stretching from 2 million years before present (BP) to 10,000 years BP.

## Submergent coasts

Introductory points:

- towards the end of the Pleistocene, about 25,000 years ago, sea level began to rise to its present level — a period known as the Flandrian Transgression — a total rise of 90 m
- this was due to an increase in global temperatures, and hence more melting of ice caps and glaciers
- this led to the creation of a number of landforms (Table 4)
- all of these landforms are being modified by current wave processes, weathering and mass movement

- as global temperatures rise due to climate change and as sea levels continue to rise:
  - □ water depth in rias and fjords will increase, leading to more erosion
  - □ shingle beaches will be more affected by storm events

Table 4 Characteristics of rias, fjords and shingle beaches

| Rias | Fjords | Shingle beaches |
|---|---|---|
| ■ submerged, winding river valleys with long fingers of water stretching inland, including their tributary valleys<br>■ widest and deepest nearer to the sea, becoming progressively narrower and shallower inland<br>■ tidal changes often reveal extensive areas of mudflats | ■ submerged, straight, glaciated valleys, with right-angled tributary valleys<br>■ have a shallower area at the mouth (a rock threshold) where glacial ice thinned as it reached the sea and hence lost its erosional power have the typical steep-sided and deep (over 1000 m) cross-profile associated with glacial troughs<br>■ can stretch many kilometres inland | ■ are features of both a fall and a rise of past sea levels<br>■ when sea level fell, sediment from the land was deposited by rivers on the newly exposed land<br>■ as sea levels rose again, this sediment was pushed landward, forming large shingle beaches, e.g. Chesil Beach in Dorset |

## Do you know?

1 Give two reasons why temperature change causes sea level change.
2 Make a list of coastal landforms resulting from sea level change.

# 1.4 Human activity

## You need to know

- a range of human activities that may impact on coastal landscapes
- how one human activity can have an intentional impact on a coastal landscape
- how one human activity can have an unintentional impact on a coastal landscape

## Impacts of human activity on coastal landscapes

A wide range of human activities take place on coasts:
- some have intentional effects on landscapes (e.g. coastal management)
- some have unintentional effects (e.g. economic developments)

Coastal management can include:

- **hard engineering**, e.g. sea walls, groynes, rip-rap and/or revetments and/or gabions
- **soft engineering**, e.g. offshore dredging and beach nourishment, dune regeneration, marsh creation

Economic developments can include:

- creation/expansion of a port, including the construction of a new breakwater
- tourist-related development
- industrial development, e.g. a power station

## Case study: Intentional activity

For this part of the specification, you are required to have **one** case study of a **coastal landscape that is being managed**.

For your case study, you should be able to describe and explain:

- the management strategy being implemented and the reason for its implementation
- the intentional impacts on the processes and flows of material and/or energy through the coastal system — this might relate to the sediment budget
- the effect of these impacts on changing coastal landforms — e.g. changes to a beach profile
- the consequence of these changes for the landscape, e.g. changing a number of landforms, or broad, more generic changes, e.g. the extension of the coastal landscape seawards

You should know:

- the name, location and approximate scale of the management strategy
- the date(s) of its implementation
- the processes and flows affected by the strategy, with supporting data
- the changes that occurred to coastal landforms and landscape
- the timescale over which the changes occurred

## Case study: Unintentional activity

For this part of the specification, you are required to have **one** case study of a **coastal landscape that is being used by people**.

For your case study, you should be able to describe and explain:

- the economic activity taking place and the reasons for it taking place
- the unintentional impacts on processes and flows of material and/or energy through the coastal system, such as disturbance to the sediment budget
- the effect of these impacts on changing coastal landforms — this might include changes to rates of erosion and/or deposition

### Key terms

**Hard engineering** A form of coastal management that involves the construction of man-made features.

**Soft engineering** A form of coastal management that involves working with nature and natural features.

### Exam tips

- This case study could be the same coastal landscape that you used for a high energy or low energy coastline (page 15), or a completely different one.
- Further examples include Studland or Sandbanks (Dorset), Holderness (Yorkshire) or Santa Barbara (California, USA).

### Exam tips

- This case study could be the same coastal landscape that you used for a high energy or low energy coastline (page 15), or a completely different one.
- Possible examples include the development of Felixstowe as a container port, the development of natural gas terminals in eastern England and south Wales, and the extraction of sand at Pakiri (New Zealand).

■ the consequence of these changes on the landscape, e.g. changing a number of landforms, or broad, more generic changes, e.g. the retreat of the coastal landscape or the resulting need for coastal management

You should know:

■ the type, location and approximate scale of the economic development
■ the date(s) of its development
■ the processes and flows affected by the development, with supporting data
■ the changes that occurred to coastal landforms and landscape
■ the timescale over which the changes occurred

## Do you know?

1 Which type of hard engineering interferes most with longshore drift?
2 Compare hard and soft engineering in general terms.
3 Describe one area where beach nourishment has taken place with beneficial effects.
4 Describe one area where beach nourishment has taken place with negative effects.

## End of section 1 questions

1 Outline the role of wind in affecting coastal energy.
2 Outline how the coast is described as a natural system.
3 Explain how tides are created.
4 Explain the formation of tombolos.
5 Assess the importance of different sources of energy in the creation of coastal landscapes.
6 Evaluate the role of sea level change over the last 25,000 years in the development of coastal landscapes.
7 Explain the influence of sea level rise and geomorphic processes in the formation of rias.
8 Hard engineering has been used intentionally to protect some coasts. With reference to a case study, explain how hard engineering can protect the coast and comment on its effectiveness.
9 'Human activity influences coastal landscape systems more than physical factors.' To what extent do you agree with this view?
10 Assess the extent to which human activity has **unintentionally** rather than **intentionally** caused change within coastal landscape systems.

# 2 Earth's life support systems

## 2.1 Water, carbon and life on Earth

**You need to know**

- water and carbon support life on Earth and move between the land, oceans and atmosphere
- the carbon and water cycles are systems with inputs, outputs and stores
- the carbon and water cycles have distinctive processes and pathways

## Water

Water is important in supporting life on Earth because it:

- supports all forms of life — all living organisms (flora, fauna and humans) comprise over 60% water
- carries substances in and out of all living cells, and supports plant tissues
- maintains the correct living requirements for all fauna and humans — without water we would die very quickly
- helps regulate surface temperatures — over 70% of the Earth's surface is covered by water, and these oceans absorb, store, transport and release heat
- helps to maintain atmospheric temperatures — clouds reflect and absorb 20% of insolation, and water vapour also absorbs outgoing long-wave radiation as part of the natural greenhouse effect
- is used in a wide range of economic activities — growing food, power generation, manufacturing, leisure activities and waste disposal

## Carbon

Carbon is also an important element because it:

- occurs in mineral form (in rocks, e.g. limestones), in living form (animals) and as a gas (e.g. $CO_2$ and methane — both GHGs)
- forms the building block for much of the natural world
- provides the basis of most of the world's energy supply — wood and fossil fuels

### Key terms

**Insolation** Incoming solar radiation.

**Greenhouse effect** The natural process whereby outgoing thermal radiation is trapped by atmospheric gases such as water vapour and $CO_2$.

**GHG** Greenhouse gas.

**Fossil fuels** Coal, oil and natural gas — they contain high proportions of carbon.

■ provides a major raw material for a wide range of manufactured products — plastics, petrol, paints, artificial fabrics

# Water and carbon cycling

Key points:
■ water and carbon are cycled between the land, oceans and atmosphere through open and closed systems
■ open systems (e.g. drainage basins) allow energy and materials to move in or out of them
■ closed systems (e.g. planet Earth) allow energy to move either in or out
■ all systems have common features (Table 5)

Table 5 Characteristics of systems

| Inputs | Outputs | Stores | Transfers or flows |
|--------|---------|--------|--------------------|
| Elements that enter a system to be processed | Outcome(s) of processing within the system | Amounts of energy or matter held, and not transferred until the appropriate processes are in place to move them | Movements of energy or matter through the system that enable inputs to become outputs |

# Systems

## Water stores

Key features (Figure 6):
■ of the world's water, 97% is saline sea water
■ almost 80% of total fresh water is locked up in ice and glaciers
■ another 20% of fresh water is in the ground
■ surface fresh water sources, such as rivers and lakes, constitute only about 1/150th of 1% of total water

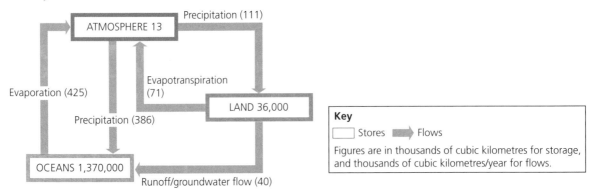

Figure 6 The global water cycle: stores and annual flows

The hydrosphere:
■ oceans hold the vast majority of all water on Earth
■ oceans supply about 90% of the evaporated water that goes into the water cycle

The atmosphere:
- contains a very small store of water (0.001% of the Earth's total water)
- is the main vector that moves water around the globe

The cryosphere:
- Antarctica holds almost 90% of the global ice mass
- the Greenland ice cap contains 10% of the total global ice mass
- ice caps and glaciers collectively cover about 10% of the Earth's surface
- **ice shelves** in Antarctica cover over 1.6 million km² (the size of Greenland), and cover 11% of its total area
- sea ice (frozen sea water) surrounds several polar regions of the world — on average sea ice covers up to 25 million km² (2.5 times the size of Canada)

The lithosphere:
- surface fresh water (glaciers, rivers, streams, lakes, reservoirs and wetlands) represents about 2.5% of all water on Earth
- 20% of all accessible surface fresh water is in Lake Baikal (Russia)
- another 20% is stored in the Great Lakes of North America
- rivers hold only about 0.006% of total fresh water reserves
- large quantities of water are also held deep underground in **aquifers**
- water from aquifers can take thousands of years to move back to the surface, if at all

> **Exam tip**
>
> It is important that proportions, or percentages, of relative amounts of water are learnt and understood in this section.

> **Key terms**
>
> **Ice shelf** A floating extension of land ice.
>
> **Aquifer** A permeable rock that can store and transmit water.

> **Exam tip**
>
> Questions will make use of the terms *lithosphere*, *hydrosphere*, *cryosphere* and *atmosphere*. Make sure you do not get them confused.

# Carbon stores

Key features (Figure 7):

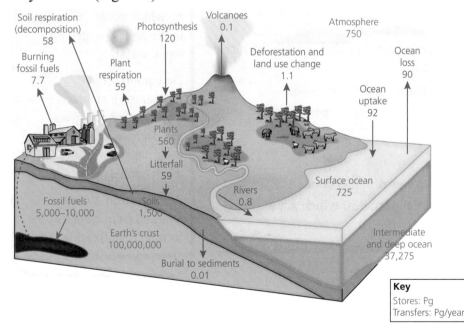

Figure 7 **The carbon cycle**

- most of Earth's carbon (99%) — over 100 million petagrams (PgC) — is stored in the lithosphere
- much of this is in fossil fuel rocks (coal and oil) and limestones
- the remainder is in the hydrosphere (38,000 PgC), the atmosphere (750 PgC), the biosphere (3000 PgC), and the cryosphere (mostly within the permafrost, amount unknown)
- carbon flows between each of these stores (or sinks) in a complex set of exchanges
- any change that shifts carbon out of one store puts more carbon in another store(s)

# Water inputs, outputs and flows

See Figure 6 (page 22).

Evaporation:

- heat (energy) is necessary for evaporation to occur — it is used to break the bonds that hold water molecules together
- this is why water easily evaporates at the boiling point (100°C) and evaporates much more slowly at freezing point
- evaporation from the oceans is the primary mechanism supporting the surface-to-atmosphere transfer of water

Evapotranspiration:

- this is the combined water loss to the atmosphere by evaporation (90%) from the ground surface and capillary fringe of the water table, and the transpiration of groundwater by plants (10%) whose roots tap the capillary fringe of the water table — water is lost from a plant through the stomata in its leaves

Condensation and cloud formation:

- condensation occurs when saturated air is cooled, usually by a rise in altitude, to below the dew point
- condensation is responsible for the formation of clouds
- clouds may produce precipitation — a route by which water returns to the Earth's surface

Precipitation:

- precipitation occurs when tiny water droplets condense on microscopic dust, salt or smoke particles, which act as condensation nuclei
- droplets may grow due to additional condensation of water vapour or when the droplets collide

## Exam tip

The units of the carbon cycle can be confusing. This should help: 1 petagram of carbon per year (1 PgC y$^{-1}$) = 1 gigatonne per year (1 GtC y$^{-1}$) = 1 billion (10$^9$) tonnes per year = 10$^{15}$ grams of carbon per year

Make sure you are consistent in your use of units.

## Key terms

**Evaporation** The process by which water changes from a liquid to a gas or vapour.

**Evapotranspiration** The combined water gain by the atmosphere through evaporation (90%) and transpiration (10%).

**Condensation** The process by which water vapour in the air is changed into liquid water.

**Dew point** The temperature at which a body of air at a given atmospheric pressure becomes fully saturated when cooled.

**Precipitation** Water released from clouds in the form of rain, freezing rain, sleet, snow or hail.

- if enough collisions occur to produce a droplet with a fall velocity that exceeds the cloud updraft speed, it will fall out of the cloud as precipitation
- another mechanism (the Bergeron–Findeisen process) leads to the rapid growth of ice crystals at the expense of the water vapour present in a cloud; these crystals fall as snow, and melt to become rain

Snow melt (ablation) and runoff:
- runoff from snowmelt varies in importance both geographically and over time
- in areas with colder climates, much springtime flow in rivers is attributable to melting snow and ice

# Carbon inputs, outputs and flows

**Weathering:**
- Atmospheric $CO_2$ combines with water vapour to form a weak carbonic acid that falls as precipitation (rain).
- This acid dissolves rocks (chemical weathering) and releases calcium magnesium, potassium and sodium ions.
- Plants, through their growth, also break up surface granites.
- Microorganisms hasten the weathering with enzymes and organic acids in the soil coupled with the carbonic acid.

Natural **sequestration** in oceans and sediments: see Figure 8:

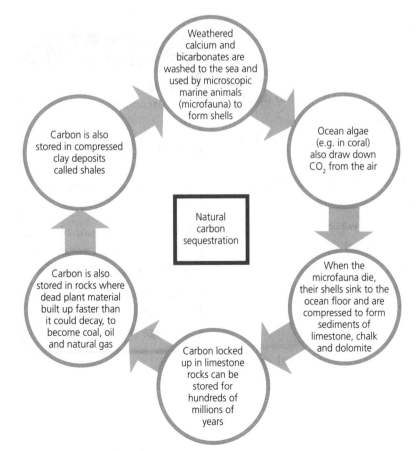

**Figure 8 Natural carbon sequestration**

Photosynthesis, respiration, decomposition and combustion:
- Plants and phytoplankton are key components of the carbon cycle.
- During photosynthesis, plants absorb $CO_2$ and sunlight to create glucose and other sugars for building plant structures.
- Phytoplankton also take $CO_2$ from the atmosphere by absorbing it into their cells.
- Using energy from the sun, both plants and phytoplankton combine $CO_2$ and water to from carbohydrate ($CH_2O$) and oxygen.

Carbon can be returned to the atmosphere by:
- respiration — plants break down the carbohydrate to get the energy they need to grow; animals (and people) eat the plants (plankton), and break down the sugar to get energy
- decomposition — plants and plankton die, decay, and are eaten by bacteria at the end of the growing season
- combustion — natural fire consumes plants

For each of these three processes the $CO_2$ released in the reaction ends up in the atmosphere.

# Other processes and pathways
## Water

The drainage basin (or catchment) hydrological cycle (Figure 9) allows the water cycle to be examined at a local scale.

- inputs include energy from the sun and precipitation
- outputs include evapotranspiration, water percolating into deep groundwater stores and runoff into the sea
- stores take place on vegetation, on the ground, in the soil and in underlying bedrock
- transfers take place between any of these stores and ultimately into the channels of the rivers of the drainage basin
- drainage basins are bounded by high land (watershed), beyond which any precipitation falls into the adjacent drainage basin
- all flows lead water to the nearest river
- the river transfers water by its channel flow to the sea — measured by its discharge
- discharge is calculated by the following:

$$\text{discharge } (Q) = \text{average velocity } (V) \times \text{cross-sectional area } (A)$$

  □ the unit is cumecs, measured in $m^3 s^{-1}$

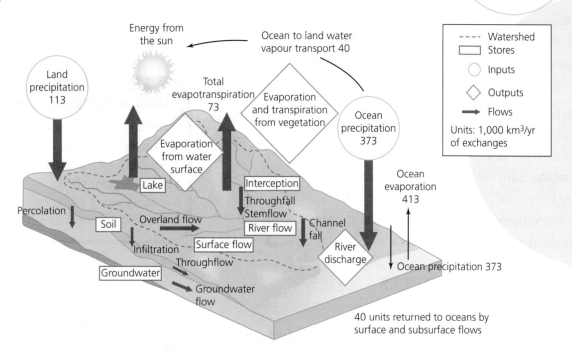

**Figure 9 The drainage basin hydrological cycle**

Stores and flows in a drainage basin (Figure 9):

■ groundwater flow — the movement of groundwater; this is the slowest transfer of water within the drainage basin and provides water for a river during drought

■ groundwater store — water that collects underground in pore spaces in rock

■ infiltration — the movement of water from the surface downwards into the soil

■ interception — the process by which precipitation is prevented from reaching the soil by the leaves and branches of trees as well as by plants and grasses

■ overland flow — the movement of water over saturated or impermeable land

■ percolation — the downward movement of water from soil into the rock below or within rock

■ stemflow — the water that runs down the stems and trunks of plants and trees to the ground

■ throughfall — the water that drips off leaves during a rainstorm

■ throughflow — the water that moves down-slope through soil

### Exam tip

You should be able to consider the factors that affect each of these flows and stores. For example, infiltration is affected by the rate of precipitation, soil type, antecedent rainfall, vegetation cover and slope.

## Carbon: natural variations

Wildfires:

■ can be caused by lightning strikes — only 10% of wildfires are started this way

■ most are started by humans, but go out of control

■ forest fires can release more carbon into the atmosphere than forests can capture

- every year wildfires burn 4 million km² of the Earth's land area, and release tonnes of $CO_2$ into the atmosphere
- new vegetation then moves on to the burned land and re-absorbs much of the $CO_2$ that the fire released

Volcanic activity:
- carbon is emitted to the atmosphere through volcanoes — about 0.1 Pg of $CO_2$ per year
- during subduction, heated rock recombines into silicate minerals, releasing $CO_2$
- when volcanoes erupt, they vent the gas to the atmosphere and cover the land with fresh silicate rock

## Carbon: human impacts

Hydrocarbon fuel extraction and burning:
- people have influenced the carbon cycle where fossil fuels have been mined and subsequently burnt
- fossil fuels range from volatile materials with low carbon-to-hydrogen ratios such as methane, to liquid petroleum and to non-volatile materials composed of almost pure carbon, such as anthracite coal
- $CO_2$ is a GHG that enhances atmospheric heating and contributes to climate change — a major environmental concern

### Key term

Subduction The process of one tectonic plate sinking beneath another at a convergent plate boundary along a sloping line called a Benioff zone.

### Exam tip

The impact of increased concentrations of $CO_2$ on world climate is well documented, though people disagree on the scale of this impact. Keep up to date on this topic.

### Do you know?

1 What are the differences between sea ice and an ice shelf?
2 Identify and explain the factors that determine transpiration rates.
3 Explain two ways in which overland flow is created.
4 Evaluate the role of volcanoes in the carbon cycle.
5 Outline two other forms of natural sequestration.

# 2.2 Water and carbon in contrasting locations

### You need to know
- how physical and human factors affect the water and carbon cycles in a tropical rainforest
- how physical and human factors affect the water and carbon cycles in an Arctic tundra area

# Case studies

For this part of the specification you are required to have studied **two** case studies, one a **tropical rainforest area** and the other an area in the **Arctic tundra**.

Your case studies must illustrate:

■ the specific water and carbon cycles operating in each location
■ the range of factors that influence the water and carbon cycles
■ the role of human activities operating in each location

For each location you should be able to describe and explain:

■ the rates of flow of water and carbon and the distinct stores of water and carbon
■ the physical factors affecting the flows and stores in the water cycle, including temperature, rock permeability and porosity, and relief
■ the physical factors affecting the flows and stores in the carbon cycle, including temperature, vegetation, organic matter in the soil and the mineral composition of rocks

## Case study: Tropical rainforest

You should be able to describe and explain for the tropical rainforest location (e.g. the Amazon):

■ in the context of one drainage basin, changes to the flows and stores within the water cycle caused by natural and human factors such as deforestation and farming
■ the impacts of human activities such as deforestation and farming on flows of carbon and stores of carbon in the soil and nutrient stores
■ strategies to manage the location that have positive effects on the water and carbon cycles, such as afforestation and various agricultural techniques, e.g. growing crops and/or livestock operations

The following sections provide some guidance.

### Background

Key points:

■ the Amazon rainforest lies within the equatorial climate zone and covers an area of some 8.2 million km², mainly in Brazil
■ the Amazon River flows through the basin from its source high in the Andes mountains towards its mouth in the Atlantic Ocean
■ it is the largest single source of fresh water runoff on Earth, representing 15–20% of global river discharge
■ at present, the Amazon rainforest acts as a carbon sink; it absorbs around 35% of the world's annual $CO_2$ emissions and produces more than 20% of the world's oxygen

### The water cycle, the carbon cycle and climate change

Table 6 shows the water cycle, the carbon cycle and climate change in the Amazon.

Table 6 The Amazon: the water cycle, the carbon cycle and climate change

| Water cycle and climate change | Carbon cycle and climate change |
|---|---|
| ■ an increase in atmospheric temperature of 2°C by 2100 will result in increased rates of evapotranspiration<br>■ sea temperatures are expected to warm too, particularly in the Pacific Ocean — the ENSO may occur more frequently<br>■ a decrease in precipitation during the dry season inland — reduced rainfall and prolonged drought are features of an ENSO year<br>■ there will be more intense rainfall during the wet season | ■ 40% of plant species may become unviable in the Amazon by 2050 — large areas of the tropical rainforest may be succeeded by mixed forest and savanna grassland, creating a reduction in the net carbon store of the rainforest<br>■ as the dry season lengthens, trees will have more time to dry out so there will be an increased incidence of wildfires, which will increase $CO_2$ emissions<br>■ forest die-back and wildfires are predicted to result in the Amazon region becoming a net source of $CO_2$, rather than a carbon sink |
| ■ sea levels are currently rising by 5 mm per annum within the Amazon delta — increased erosion and flooding is likely to have a substantial impact on low-lying areas and will destroy the coastal mangrove forests<br>■ glaciers in the Andes provide the source for 50% of the discharge of the upper Amazon — over the last 30 years, Peruvian glaciers have shrunk by 20% and it is predicted that Peru will lose all glaciers below a height of 6000 m by 2050 | ■ Amazonian soils under rainforest contain up to $9\,kg\,m^{-2}$ of carbon in the upper 50 cm of the soil profile<br>■ clearance of the rainforest for farming and ranching will result in less carbon stored in the soil — afforestation is unlikely<br>■ there is little sign of any positive effects from management strategies |

## Case study: Arctic tundra

You should be able to describe and explain for the Arctic tundra location (e.g. northern Alaska and Canada):
■ seasonal changes in the water and carbon cycles
■ the impacts of the developing oil and gas industries on the water and carbon cycles
■ strategies to manage and moderate impacts of the oil and gas industries

The following sections provide some guidance.

### Background

Key points:
■ 50% of the land in northern Alaska and Canada is underlain by permafrost

- in the coldest parts it is hundreds of metres thick, whereas further south there may be only a few metres of frozen soil
- in the southern parts, soil thaws on the surface a little during summer — a metre or so in depth (called the active layer)
- soils of the permafrost are crammed with un-degraded, well-preserved organic matter in the form of leaves, twigs, roots — this is an enormous store of inert carbon (900 Gt)
- permafrost causes considerable problems for economic activities:
  - in construction, the elasticity of ice reduces the effectiveness of explosives used in excavating
  - structures need to be insulated from the ground so that the soil does not melt and sag or move under it
  - paved roads or runways must have insulation beneath them
  - other than grazing, farming is impossible

## The water cycle, the carbon cycle and climate change

Table 7 shows the water cycle, the carbon cycle and climate change in the Arctic.

**Table 7 The Arctic: the water cycle, the carbon cycle and climate change**

| Nature of change | Impacts of change |
|---|---|
| - scientists have measured a retreat in the permafrost zone as climate warming has increased<br>- this is particularly acute in northern Alaska and northwest Canada<br>- increases in temperature of only 1°C have led to the thaw rate trebling<br>- current evidence indicates that around Prudhoe Bay on the North Slope, the permafrost will not just warm up but will thaw completely by about 2070–80<br>- permafrost under the sea bed is also thawing | - slumping and landslides are common; buildings become undermined, roads subside unevenly and crack; the supports holding pipelines shift and even crack the pipeline<br>- given the world's dependence on oil and gas, the threat of pipelines being shut down is significant<br>- the melting of permafrost creates very wet ground and releases organic carbon, mainly as methane<br>- the melting of the permafrost releases a lot of water on to the surface, creating a series of lakes that cannot drain because of the frozen and impermeable soils beneath them<br>- while engineering can prevent the thawing of permafrost underneath important structures, there is little that can be done to prevent the general melting of the layer<br>- bubbles of methane (methane fountains) are rising from the sea bed |

### Exam tip

Ensure you support your answers with references to places clearly located in an area of Arctic tundra. Note: Antarctica is not relevant here.

### Do you know?

1 Describe the impact of climate change on the climate of the Amazon.
2 Outline the impact of climate change on the biosphere of the Amazon.
3 Describe the distribution of permafrost in the northern hemisphere.
4 Outline the mechanisms by which GHGs are emitted in the tundra.

# 2.3 Changes in the water and carbon cycles

## You need to know

- human factors can both disturb and enhance the water and carbon cycles
- the pathways and processes that control the water and carbon cycles change over time

## Human factors

Key points:

- systems operate to achieve a state of dynamic equilibrium
- this can be upset:
  - □ for the water cycle — by intense rain in a drainage basin leading to more water in the stores (rivers and lakes), which may overflow or flood
  - □ for the carbon cycle — by the growth of plants in summer decreasing the amount of $CO_2$ in the atmosphere as photosynthesis takes place
  - □ by a range of human activities (see below)

## Human activity and the water cycle

Table 8 shows human factors that are affecting the water cycle.

Table 8 Human factors affecting the water cycle

### Key terms

**Dynamic equilibrium** The balanced state of a system when opposing forces, or inputs and outputs, are equal.

**Deforestation** The clearance of forests for agriculture or pasture.

**Afforestation** The planting of trees on previously un-forested land.

**Artesian basin** An aquifer located in a basin-like geological structure (called a syncline).

| Factor | Commentary |
|---|---|
| Deforestation and afforestation | <ul><li>deforestation removes water-absorbent forests, which trap and transpire rainfall, and replaces them with farmland; this significantly increases both the volume of water reaching a river and the speed with which it travels</li><li>afforestation has the opposite effect — it increases interception and reduces overland flow</li></ul> |
| Land-use change (rural, farming) | <ul><li>converting arable land to pastoral land increases compaction by livestock and creates more overland flow</li><li>converting pastoral land to arable land increases infiltration, although use of heavy machinery compacts soil locally</li></ul> |
| Land-use change (urban growth) | <ul><li>urban growth creates impermeable surfaces (concrete, tarmac) and this reduces infiltration</li><li>urban drainage systems deliver rainwater to rivers more quickly, increasing flood risk</li></ul> |
| Water storage | <ul><li>reservoirs reduce river flows by holding back water</li></ul> |
| Water abstraction | <ul><li>people make use of the water in aquifers and artesian basins — in some places they pump water out faster than nature replenishes it</li><li>the water table can be lowered by excessive pumping — wells can 'go dry' and become useless</li><li>people also take water from surface rivers, which reduces their flow</li></ul> |

# Human activity and the carbon cycle

Farming practices:

■ tillage of cropland soils can cause them to lose carbon — it ‚ increases aeration and soil temperatures, making organic material more available for decomposition

■ crop rotation, residue management, reduction of soil erosion and improvement of irrigation can increase carbon levels in soils

■ rice cultivation and livestock farming are two sources of methane — alteration of rice cultivation practices and changes to livestock feed are therefore potential management practices that could reduce methane sources

Deforestation:

■ see Figure 10

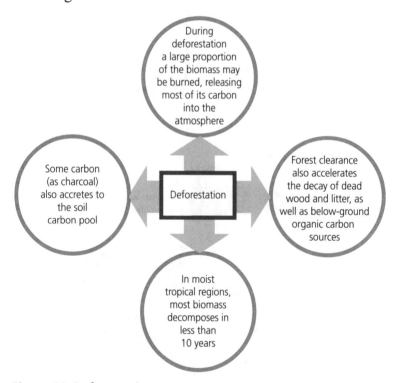

**Figure 10 Deforestation**

Afforestation:

■ forests are capable of sequestering carbon — up to 200 tonnes of carbon per hectare in a mature forest in the UK

■ forest soils are capable of holding more than twice this amount of carbon

■ afforestation is therefore an effective form of carbon storage

Fossil fuel combustion:

■ the burning of fossil fuels produces around 21 Pg of $CO_2$ per year, but natural processes can absorb only a proportion, resulting in a net increase of 8.5 Pg of atmospheric $CO_2$ per year

- concentrations of $CO_2$ gas in the atmosphere have increased from 280 parts per million (ppm) in 1750 to over 400 ppm at present
- the burning of fossil fuels is the main cause of the enhanced greenhouse effect
- urban areas are zones of concentration of carbon emissions, through combustion and industrial processes, e.g. cement manufacture

Carbon sequestration by humans can be achieved by carbon capture and storage:

- it can be applied to power stations and industry with accessible deep sea or geological burial sites
- supporters say it removes the problem at source
- those opposed state it encourages the continued use of fossil fuels
- no effective large-scale scheme currently exists

## Feedback

There are two types of feedback (Figure 11):

- positive feedback is where a change causes a further, or snowball, effect, continuing or even accelerating the original change
- negative feedback acts to lessen the effect of the original change and ultimately to reverse it

> ### Key terms
>
> **Enhanced greenhouse effect** The increased impact of greater amounts of GHGs ($CO_2$ and methane) caused by human activity.
>
> **Carbon capture and storage (CCS)** The separation of $CO_2$ from waste gases in power stations, and then storing it deep underground.
>
> **Feedback** Occurs when one of the elements of the system changes, such as an input. The state of the store changes and the equilibrium is upset.

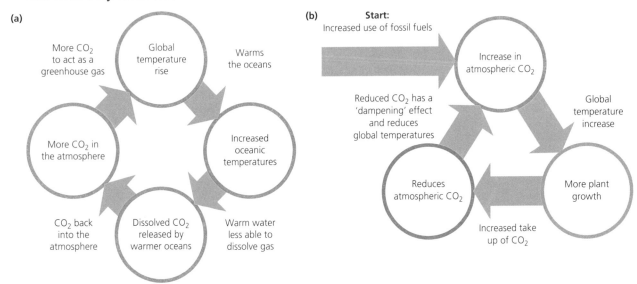

**Figure 11** Examples of feedback loops in natural systems: (a) positive feedback between the water and carbon cycles, (b) negative feedback in the carbon cycle

# Changes over time

## Short term

Diurnal changes in the water cycle:

- evapotranspiration reduces at night and increases during the day
- in tropical areas, rainfall is often higher in the afternoon due to convection

> ### Key term
>
> **Diurnal** Changes over a 24-hour period.

Diurnal changes in the carbon cycle:
- photosynthesis is greater by day than by night
- electricity production in power stations increases in the late afternoon/early evening

Seasonal changes in the water cycle:
- evapotranspiration is greater in summer than in winter
- rainfall patterns are affected by seasonality, e.g. monsoon rains in southeast Asia
- snowmelt in tundra areas increases the discharge of rivers in spring

Seasonal changes in the carbon cycle:
- changes in **net primary productivity** show that the growing season is when most carbon flows from the atmosphere to plants
- for the rainforests, this period is all year round
- for all other ecosystems (on land and in the sea), the growing season is when temperatures are warmer and days are longer — i.e. the summer

> **Key term**
>
> **Net primary productivity (NPP)** The amount of organic matter that is available to humans and animals to harvest and consume.

# Long term

The specification defines 'long term' as meaning as millions of years.

For the water cycle:
- the main changes have concerned the periods of ice advance (glacial) followed by periods of ice retreat (inter-glacial)
- the last major ice advance in the northern hemisphere occurred 20,000 years ago — some scientists state we are currently in an inter-glacial
- sea level falls during a glacial and rises during an inter-glacial

For the carbon cycle:
- carbon locked up in carbonate rocks can be stored for millions, or even hundreds of millions, of years
- carbon seeps out from active volcanoes, and was released when new fold mountain chains (e.g. the Himalayas) were created
- carbon flows changed during glacial periods:
  - □ more $CO_2$ was absorbed by the cooler oceans; phytoplankton growth increased and when they died they sank to the ocean floor, taking carbon into sediments
  - □ on land, more carbon was sequestered into the permafrost, which is now at risk of being released (see Arctic tundra, page 30)
- during inter-glacials atmospheric $CO_2$ levels increase and NPP increases as photosynthesis increases

> **Exam tip**
>
> Ensure that you understand the differences between short-term and long-term changes in both the water and carbon cycles.

## Monitoring change

Key points:
- research into, and monitoring of, changes in the water and carbon cycles is important in the understanding of climate change
- NASA and NOAA use satellite technology to monitor the extent and thickness of ice caps and sheets as well as to monitor surface temperatures and atmospheric composition
- nuclear submarines also monitor ice sheets from below

### Do you know?

1 Explain how the enhanced greenhouse effect operates.
2 Outline two other forms of human-induced sequestration.
3 Explain how carbon exploitation (such as in power stations) and carbon capture can work together.
4 Explain the difference between negative and positive feedback mechanisms.
5 Why are short-term changes in the water cycle important to humans?

# 2.4 Links between the water and carbon cycles

### You need to know
- the water and carbon cycles are interlinked
- the global implications of water and carbon management

## Linkages

Some key points:
- Atmosphere — $CO_2$ is exchanged between the atmosphere and vegetation on land and phytoplankton at sea by a variety of processes; water is also exchanged with the oceans and land
- Oceans (hydrosphere) — as atmospheric $CO_2$ levels increase, global temperatures rise and warmer seas absorb less $CO_2$, evaporation rates increase and thermal expansion of the oceans occurs
- Cryosphere — as global temperatures rise (due to increased atmospheric $CO_2$) there is more melting of ice; sea levels rise; the thawing of permafrost releases more $CO_2$ and methane

- Vegetation (biosphere) — as temperatures rise, rates of photosynthesis increase with more NPP

Most scientists agree that all of these linkages are connected to climate change, which will have a significant impact on life on Earth.

# Human activity

Table 9 shows human activity and change in the availability of water and carbon.

Table 9 Human activity and change in the availability of water and carbon

| Factors — water | Factors — carbon |
|---|---|
| <ul><li>population growth and rising living standards</li><li>increased expectations of water use — washing machines, dishwashers, private swimming pools</li><li>industrial development in the emerging economies (e.g. China and India)</li><li>new energy developments, e.g. fracking, may contaminate water stocks</li><li>increased use of irrigation</li><li>contamination of surface and groundwater supplies by domestic, industrial and agricultural activities</li><li>over-abstraction of water from rivers and groundwater (aquifers)</li></ul> | <ul><li>population growth and rising living standards</li><li>industrial development in the emerging economies (e.g. China and India)</li><li>attitudes to energy use (public perception) determine rates of energy use and wastage</li><li>responses to climate — greater use of energy to heat or cool depending on external weather conditions</li><li>environmental priorities — there are varying attitudes to the cost to the environment vs the need for cheap energy</li><li>land-use changes, e.g. ranching increases carbon emissions</li></ul> |

# Climate change

The key links between, and impacts of, long-term climate change and the water and carbon cycles are:

- changes in the carbon cycle are the causes of climate change through the combination of the greenhouse and enhanced greenhouse effects
- climate change is impacting on both the water and carbon cycles

The water cycle:

- climate change is having, and will continue to have, effects on the water cycle, such as more evaporation and/or more precipitation in some regions
- more incidence of flooding is also likely in some areas, although there will be more drought in others
- extreme weather events, e.g. storms, are more likely

The carbon cycle:

- climate change is having, and will continue to have, effects on the carbon cycle, such as the release of more $CO_2$ from permafrost areas as they warm
- processes such as decomposition and photosynthesis will increase in some areas
- **ocean acidification** is also likely to increase, impacting negatively on coral reefs

## Exam tip

Support some of these points by referring to examples of where the availability of water/carbon has been affected.

## Key term

**Ocean acidification** Involves a decrease in the pH of the oceans caused by the uptake of $CO_2$ (from fossil fuel combustion) from the atmosphere.

■ humans have to either **adapt** to the water cycle-related outcomes of climate change (increased rates of ice cap melting, flooding and drought) or **mitigate** these impacts by managing the carbon cycle, or both

# Management strategies
## Carbon

Table 10 shows some strategies for carbon reduction.

Table 10 Carbon-reduction strategies

| Strategy | Nature | Commentary |
|---|---|---|
| Afforestation | Planting trees on previously unforested land | ■ increases carbon sequestration and reduces flood risk |
| Wetland restoration | Conversion of wetlands back to their original state — may be part of flood-management or RAMSAR schemes | ■ when wetlands are drained, soils become exposed to oxygen and carbon stocks, which are resistant to decay under the anaerobic conditions prevalent in wetland soils, can be lost by aerobic respiration<br>■ restoration stops this |
| Improving agricultural practices | Drought-tolerant crops; no-tillage systems; selective irrigation systems; mulching; crop rotation; more 'indoor' farming; GM farming | ■ much of the technology already exists and GM farming is used in many parts of the world to create resistant strains of rice and soya<br>■ costs are prohibitive in the developing world, where the need is greatest<br>■ GM farming is subject to debate<br>■ high energy costs for 'indoor' farming |
| Carbon trading | Principle of 'polluter pays'; the EU has EUETS — a mechanism that sets limits (caps) on the emission of a pollutant and allows companies that are within the limit to sell credits (trade) to companies that need to pollute more | ■ the power generation, steel, cement and airline industries are part of the scheme<br>■ any EU-based industry can buy or sell credits, whether it is a company covered by the EUETS or not<br>■ trading can be done directly between buyers and sellers, through several organised exchanges or through the many intermediaries active in the carbon market |

The international agreements of the Kyoto Protocol (Table 11) were an intervention in the carbon cycle at a global scale:
■ it set legally binding national targets for $CO_2$ emissions compared with 1990
■ it proposed schemes to enable governments to reach these targets

## Key terms

**Adaptation** Changing lifestyles to cope with, rather than trying to stop, climate change.

**Mitigation** Reduction in the output/amount of GHGs and/or increases in carbon stores.

**RAMSAR** International Convention on Wetlands — a global conservation scheme.

**GM** Genetic modification.

**EUETS** European Union Emission Trading Scheme.

## Exam tip

You are advised to be aware of what is being done globally to reduce the impact of deforestation and land-use change. Research the work of the UN-REDD scheme.

**Table 11** Evaluation of the Kyoto Protocol

| Successes | Failures |
|---|---|
| Kyoto paved the way for new rules and measurements on low carbon legislation, e.g. the UK's Climate Change Act (2008) | Slow ratification — the UK was one of the first to do so; the USA signed the Protocol but did not ratify it, and Canada withdrew from it |
| By 2012, carbon emissions in the EU were 22% lower than in 1990, beating the initial global 5% target | By 2015 global carbon emissions had increased to 65% above 1990 levels, driven by growth in India and China |
| The Clean Development Mechanism supported 75 countries in developing less polluting technology | Complex carbon 'trading' systems were set up, and some carbon 'sinks' were allowed to offset emissions; both systems were criticised |
| Kyoto started a global approach to dealing with anthropogenic climate change. More UN conferences on climate change followed | Only industrialised countries were involved, with 'emerging' economies such as India and China left out; the USA's non-ratification has not helped |

A further conference took place in Paris in late 2015. Three of the main outcomes of the COP21 Agreement (Paris) 2015 were:

- a temperature increase of 2°C by 2100 is unacceptable — the Agreement set a maximum of 1.5°C
- GHG emissions will be allowed to rise for now, but with more sequestration aimed for later this century to keep within scientifically determined limits
- emissions targets will be set separately by countries, reviewed every 5 years and after each review, emissions levels decreased meaningfully

# Water

Table 12 shows some strategies for water management.

**Table 12  Some water-management strategies**

| Strategy | Nature | Commentary |
|---|---|---|
| Improved forestry techniques | ■ various protection schemes in the rainforests, e.g. ARPA | ■ the aim is to prevent logging, ranching and mineral exploitation |
| Improved water allocations | ■ smart irrigation — using automated spray technology and drip irrigation systems | ■ avoids the wastage of water under current systems — which also lead to waterlogging and salinisation |
| Recycling | ■ the use of greywater, and water-harvesting techniques | ■ low-cost options that produce water for agriculture but not for people<br>■ collection of water on roofs and storage in butts or tanks — for some domestic and agricultural uses and for gardens |
| Drainage-basin planning | ■ regards the drainage basin as the basic unit of water management<br>■ it is based on achieving close cooperation between users and managers within a basin | ■ the aims are to maintain environmental quality, efficient use of water resources and an equitable distribution of those resources<br>■ these aims may work within countries, but trans-boundary issues may prove more difficult |

## Key terms

**Anthropogenic** Processes and actions associated with human activity.

**ARPA** The Amazon Regional Protected Area.

**Salinisation** When potential evapotranspiration is greater than precipitation and the water table is near the ground surface, salts are drawn up through soil and deposited.

**Greywater** Water from bathroom sinks, showers, bathtubs and washing machines. It is water that has not come into contact with faeces, either from the toilet or from washing nappies.

**Trans-boundary** When countries share the same river or drainage basin.

## Exam tip

One of the main participants in setting targets is the IPCC (Intergovernmental Panel on Climate Change). Keep up to date with its reports and the outcomes from this organisation.

## Do you know?

1 Comment on the impact urban growth has on the carbon and water cycles.
2 Summarise the key features of the Kyoto Protocol.
3 What could be the benefits of warming in the Arctic?
4 Research two other outcomes of the COP21 (Paris) Agreement.

## Exam tip

No easily accessible example of drainage-basin planning currently exists — it is largely an aim at the present time.

## End of section 2 questions

1 In the context of climate change, distinguish between 'mitigation' and 'adaptation'.
2 Explain how land-use change can affect the water cycle.
3 With reference to a river catchment that you have studied, examine the impact of precipitation on drainage basin stores and transfers.
4 Examine the significance of the role of vegetation in linking the water and carbon cycles.
5 Outline the process of photosynthesis in the carbon cycle.
6 How far do you agree that changes to the carbon cycle will lead to increasingly severe storm events?
7 Assess the relative importance of natural factors in changing the size of major stores of carbon.
8 Evaluate the extent to which today's increasing demand for energy is the most important factor modifying the carbon cycle.
9 'Human activity has caused irreversible damage to the fragile inter-relationship between the water cycle and the carbon cycle.' To what extent do you agree with this view?
10 'Human factors affect the water cycle more significantly in the tropical rainforest than in the Arctic tundra.' Discuss.

# 3 Changing spaces; Making places

## 3.1 What is a place?

### You need to know
- places are multi-faceted, shaped by shifting flows and connections that change over time
- people see, experience and understand place in different ways and this changes over time
- places are represented through a variety of contrasting formal and informal agencies

### Case studies: Place profiles

You are required to have **two** case studies of **contrasting** place profiles at a **local scale**.

These must include:
- the demographic, socio-economic, cultural, political, built and natural characteristics that shape their place identity
- the past and present connections that shape place identity and embed the place in regional, national, international and global scales
- how shifting flows of people (e.g. commuter movements, migration), resources (e.g. natural deposits, technology), money and investment (e.g. funding from the EU, TNCs) and ideas (e.g. the knowledge economy) have helped shape the demographic, socio-economic and cultural profile of these places over time

### How do you assess a place profile?

A place local to you (Figure 12):
- an obvious method of exploring the character of a place local to you is by direct observation — walk through the area and look and, simultaneously, question what you see
- try to relate, interpret and assess your observations, i.e. form an opinion about 'what is good' and 'what is wrong', and map them
- identify aspects that you consider should be changed (problems or issues) and those that are very characteristic of the place and should be maintained
- engage with the place at a personal level

### Key terms

**Place profile**  A description of a place based on the combination of its characteristics.

**Local scale**  That of a village or urban neighbourhood.

### Exam tip

How large should a 'place' be? It should be one you could walk around on a one-day fieldtrip, with fewer than 20,000 people, e.g. a ward of a town.

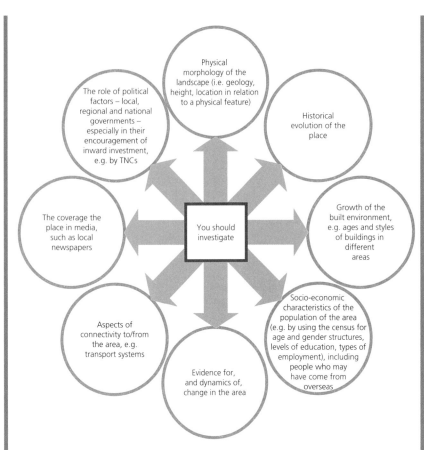

Figure 12 Local place investigation

**Exam tips**

■ Consider using online sources for socio-economic data:

Office of National Statistics (ONS): www.neighbourhood. statistics.gov.uk

DataShine maps (based on the 2011 Census): http://datashine.org.uk

Consumer Data Research Centre (CDRC) maps: http://data.cdrc.ac.uk

■ Learn some facts about your local place that support the place profile — then you may be able to make some comparative points with the contrasting place.

A 'contrasting' place:

■ should be a location with which you are unfamiliar

■ should be 'distant' from the local place in terms of character

■ may also be geographically distant, e.g. located in a different country to the local place study or in an unfamiliar part of the UK (or your home country)

■ it is equally acceptable for the contrasting place to be located near to the local place providing it illustrates the necessary contrast

The contrasting place must show significant contrast to the local place in terms of each of:

■ economic development

■ population density

■ cultural background

■ systems of political and economic organisation

## Past and present connections

The characteristics of places are influenced by:

■ forces that have operated in the past — evidenced by the ethnic composition of the population, old buildings, public spaces, street names and even the place name

■ present-day connections at regional, national, international and global scales (Table 13)

Table 13 Present-day connections that impact on the characteristics of place

| Scale | Connections |
|-------|-------------|
| Regional | ■ transport/communication links: road; rail; air; broadband<br>■ nearby urban areas: workplaces; shopping facilities; leisure activities<br>■ regional governance: e.g. Local Enterprise Partnerships; local government policies |
| National/international | ■ political attitudes and the resulting decisions<br>■ national government policies — may include impact of international trade agreements, e.g. the Common Agricultural Policy (EU) |
| Global | ■ global retailers or industries/offices?<br>■ global tourism opportunities/visitors?<br>■ twinning arrangements?<br>■ evidence of inward migration of people from overseas?<br>■ ease, or otherwise, of access to an international airport |

## Shifting flows

Several types of movement of people impact on a place profile:

■ short-term movements of people, e.g. commuters and commuting villages
■ medium-term movements of people, e.g. students to an inner city, retirees to a coastal area
■ long-term, e.g. economic migrants from one country to another, or refugees

Resources can shape a place profile by:

■ the mining of minerals, e.g. coal, gold, iron ore
■ the availability, or otherwise, of broadband
■ depletion that can devastate a community — often requiring a need for regeneration

Sources of money and investment:

■ TNCs that operate across national borders and bring **FDI** – their investment may be tied to government incentives.
■ Smaller businesses – attracted by financial incentives too, or with local connections.
■ Regional and national governments – part of wider improvements in an area, e.g. new road or rail networks.
■ Local governments, e.g. providing the infrastructure for a new industrial estate.

Ideas impact on a place profile by:

■ the development of new technologies, allowing industries and activities to develop, e.g. call-centre activity in a town

**Key term**

**FDI** Foreign Direct Investment.

- high-tech industries (e.g. in education, finance and manufacturing) can allow places to be part of the knowledge economy
- raising the status and acceptance of education *per se* and, with it, levels of aspiration

# Understanding place

## The concepts of space vs place

A space:

- has a precise position on the planet
- is usually indicated by coordinates determined by latitude and longitude

A place:

- can have an objective meaning, such as map coordinates or its location on a GPS
- is also given subjective 'meaning' by people — a sense of place
- creates an important basis of life — a 'lived experience'

The concept of place can be summarised as:

place = space + meaning

## Perceptions of place

General features:

- people perceive places in different ways — our identity influences perceptions
- the way we see a place may not be the same as the way other people see it
- age, gender, sexuality, religion and role can impact on perceptions of a place

Age:

- perceptions of a place often change through our life-cycle stages
- young adults may prefer to live in locations where work, shops and leisure facilities are close by
- people with young families may desire more space (a garden, a park), with access to a nursery or school
- older people may prefer a more secluded place

Gender:

- perhaps not as influential in developed societies as in the past, though stereotypical attitudes may prevail regarding work vs home
- some workplaces are still dominated by one gender — e.g. mining, nursing

### Key terms

**Knowledge economy** The activities that gather, store and process knowledge.

**Location** A point in space with specific links to other points in space.

**GPS** Global Positioning System.

**Sense of place** The personal feelings associated with living in a place.

**Lived experience** The actual feelings and personal history of living in a place.

**Identity** An assemblage of personal characteristics, such as gender, sexuality, race and religion.

### Exam tip

Create a list of 'places' that are important to you at a variety of scales, and why they are important to you. They will be useful to support your arguments.

### Key term

**Life-cycle stage** Describes the age and family status of a person, such as *young adult*, *married with children* or *retired*.

■ gender still impacts on the perception of 'safety' (or lack of it) in some urban areas — e.g. train carriages at night

Sexuality:
■ some cities have concentrations of LGBTQ+ groups in certain areas
■ this enhances the sense of belonging, and provides a form of security
■ there are economic benefits too, as the 'pink pound' can be an important part of regeneration

Religion:
■ some places are important for their spiritual meaning, including some mountains, rivers, volcanoes and lakes
■ religious buildings (e.g. churches, mosques, synagogues) are often central to the sense of belonging to a community, or are key sites when visiting a place

Role:
■ perceptions of place vary according to role and responsibility, which may change over the life cycle
■ the same place may even be seen in a different light within a 24-hour period, e.g. at different times of the day a city centre may be a place of work, a place to shop or a place of entertainment
■ similarly, a small park may be used by different people at different times of the day, e.g. parents with young children, teenagers, and retired members of a bowling club

## Emotional attachment

Key features:
■ emotional attachment can come with long-term association with a place — based on memories
■ people can feel attached to a place even if they no longer live there
■ for some, attachment to a place is more subjective — a 'homeland' with a strong sense of identity, but no geographical or political basis
■ diaspora in the past has led to emotional attachment by some people to places that they have never seen or visited

## Globalisation and time–space compression

Key points:
■ technological developments have taken place to create a 'shrinking world' to facilitate globalisation

**Key term**

Belonging A sense of being part of a collective identity.

**Exam tip**

Consider a town/city you know well. Think about the location of places where different groups of people might live or meet, and their reasons for doing so.

**Exam tip**

Perception is an important influence on the meanings people give to places. Make sure you have real-world examples to support several of the influences given here.

**Key terms**

Diaspora The movement of large numbers of people away from their homeland.

Globalisation The growing economic interdependence of countries worldwide through increasing volume and variety of cross-border transactions in goods and services, freer international capital flows, and more rapid and widespread diffusion of technology.

- this refers to the idea that the world feels smaller over time, because places are closer in terms of travel or contact time — known as time–space compression
- as a result, people can feel an emotional attachment to places far away — being part of a 'global village'
- some places have 'gained' from these processes (e.g. tourist resorts and financial centres), while other places have 'lost' (e.g. small-scale farmers in EDCs and old manufacturing industry areas in ACs)

# Representation of place

## Informal methods

Key points:
- several agencies make use of our imagination to influence the way we see a place
- advertising agencies combine visual and written imagery to enhance the settings of a place
- tourist boards may select aspects of a place that fit a desired perception of that place
- this representation may be informal, but it is still powerful — novels, poems, songs, the visual arts and other diverse media (television, film, video, photography) 'bring alive' different places
- in these cases we may struggle to match the factual with the fiction
- graffiti and blogs present highly individual representations of place, being strongly influenced by perceptions

## Formal methods

Key points:
- more statistical data about places are now collected, stored and analysed than ever before
- the most effective formal representations of places are often censuses
- there has been a dramatic increase in the quantity and quality of geospatial data
- many government agencies maintain websites that present formal representations of places
- formal representations offer rational perspectives of a place profile, such as numbers of people living in a place, their ages, gender and educational qualifications
- they are limited in their ability to indicate the 'lived experience' aspects of a place profile

**Key terms**

Time–space compression The notion that the cost of communicating over distance has fallen rapidly.

EDCs Emerging and developing countries.

ACs Advanced countries.

Representation of place The cultural practices by which people interpret and portray the world around them and present themselves to others.

**Exam tip**

Consider how twenty-first century advertisers entice you to tourist locations.

**Key term**

Geospatial data Locational information about a place — geographic information systems (GIS) are often used.

## Do you know?

1 Give examples of how resources influence a place profile.
2 Explain how different levels of government can impact on a place.
3 Distinguish between 'space' and 'place'.
4 Why do informal representations of place need to be interpreted with care?
5 The word 'palimpsest' is used when considering the past connections of a place. What does it mean?

# 3.2 Economic change and social inequality

## You need to know

- the distribution of resources, wealth and opportunities is not evenly spread
- processes of economic change can create opportunities for some, while creating and exacerbating social inequality for others
- social inequality impacts people and places in different ways

# Social inequality

## Factors

Social inequality can be illustrated by housing tenure:
- owner-occupiers tend to have higher levels of wealth, though that wealth can be 'locked' in the value of the property and difficult to access
- people who rent are largely on lower incomes, though that is an over-generalisation when considering the rental sector in many central areas of cities
- squatters are people with low incomes, whether in ACs, EDCs or LIDCs

Health:
- may be measured by morbidity and longevity
- there are direct links between place, employment, lifestyle and health, e.g. people in primary employment have a higher risk of poorer health and mortality
- 'food deserts' — places with a higher incidence of fast-food outlets and lower availability of fresh food — have higher rates of morbidity and are associated with low incomes

## Key terms

**Social inequality** The uneven distribution of opportunities and rewards for different social groups, defined by factors such as housing, healthcare, education, employment and access to services.

**Housing tenure** The system under which housing is occupied, e.g. renting (tenancy) and owner-occupying.

**LIDCs** Low-income developing countries.

**Morbidity** The degree of ill-health experienced by a person.

**Longevity** How long a person's life expectancy is.

- access to healthcare (e.g. clinics, hospitals) can depend on personal income, but also on provision of basics such as clean water and sanitation
- lifestyle choices are also important, such as consumption of alcohol and tobacco

Education:
- in the UK, educational provision and outcome (measured by literacy and examination success) is unequal
- outcome is strongly linked to income levels — working-class white children in poverty have the lowest educational achievement
- boys are more likely to have lower exam results than girls, especially those of Bangladeshi, Pakistani and black African origin

Employment and income:
- in the UK there is a huge disparity in incomes and cost of living, both nationally and locally; in London, some jobs pay a 'London Allowance' because of this disparity
- those working in the primary sector and low-level services (e.g. in the care industry) receive lower pay than those in more skilled and professional sectors
- seasonal and insecure employment (e.g. zero-hours contracts) usually pays less
- informal employment is common in many places in EDCs and LIDCs

Access to services:
- the number of services available
- the quality of transport links to those services
- the provision of communication systems to those services, e.g. mobile phone networks, broadband
- socio-economic factors such as income, age and gender

## Indicators

The Human Development Index (HDI):
- ranks countries according to economic criteria (GDP per capita, adjusted for PPP) and social criteria (life expectancy and literacy)
- devised by the United Nations Development Programme (UNDP) and has been used in its current form since 2010 — the three 'ingredients' are processed to produce a number between 0 and 1

The Index of Multiple Deprivation (IMD) 2015:
- published by the Department for Communities and Local Government, it informs national and local government decision-making

### Key terms

**Informal employment** Employment that is not formally recognised or recorded — involves street activity and that hidden from the authorities.

**PPP** Purchasing Power Parity — allows comparison based on the actual cost of living in a country.

- ranks the super output areas (SOAs) across England according to a combination of seven domains of deprivation: income, employment, education, health, crime, barriers to housing and services, and living environment
- each of these domains is based on a further number of indicators — 37 in total
- each indicator is based on the most recent data available, although in practice most indicators in the 2017 data, for example, relate to the tax year ending April 2015
- uses smaller parts of the SOAs called Lower SOAs (LSOAs), each of which contains about 1500 residents or about 650 households; this allows the identification of small pockets of deprivation
- the deciles shown on the IMD maps are produced by ranking 32,844 LSOAs and dividing them into 10 equal-sized groups: decile 1 represents the most deprived 10% of areas nationally, and decile 10 the least deprived 10%
- when interpreting this data, note
  - the rank of the deciles is relative; they simply show that one area is more deprived than another but not by how much
  - you will see large areas of colour, often the same or a similar shade — note that these show areas and not numbers of people living there
  - the data shown by such neighbourhood-level maps provide a description of areas as a whole and not of individuals within those areas
  - deprivation (Figure 13), not affluence, is mapped

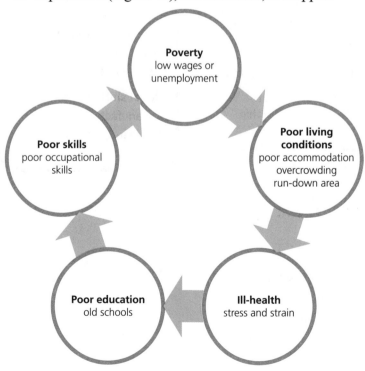

Figure 13 **The cycle of deprivation**

The Gini coefficient:

- values vary between 0 (perfect equality) and 100 (perfect inequality)
- these extremes are practically impossible, so we say that the lower the value, the more equally household income is distributed, and conversely the higher the value, the more unequally household income is distributed
- it is therefore a measure of the overall extent to which households, from the bottom of the income distribution upwards, receive less than an equal share of income

## Spatial patterns

Table 14 shows factors affecting spatial patterns of social inequality.

**Table 14** Factors affecting spatial patterns of social inequality

| Factor | Commentary |
|---|---|
| Income | <ul><li>the ability to pay for housing, goods and services affects where people live</li><li>in general, wealthier people live with other wealthy people — in the outer suburbs in ACs, and in central city areas in EDCs and LIDCs (gated communities)</li><li>in ACs poorer people may live in sink estates</li></ul> |
| Housing | <ul><li>affordability of housing is the key factor in social inequality — this is related to income and the ability to pay</li><li>low-income people tend to live in slum housing or spontaneous settlements</li><li>in some areas of ACs, the purchasing of a second home is making it difficult for locals to buy or rent a home</li></ul> |
| Health | <ul><li>sub-standard housing is associated with ill-health</li><li>access to healthcare in some rural areas may be challenging</li><li>some suggest that poorer inner-city areas have lower levels of healthcare provision than outer suburbs</li><li>for many towns the opposite is the case, as many surgeries and dentists can be found more centrally</li></ul> |
| Education | <ul><li>some suggest that there are contrasts in access to education between rural and urban areas and within urban areas (inner city vs outer suburbs)</li><li>this is a complicated area of study, however, and such generalisations are difficult to prove</li></ul> |

# Economic change
## Structural change and its impact

During the last 30 years, there has been an economic global shift mainly to Asian countries (for the processes involved, see Figure 14):

- manufacturing jobs have moved from western Europe, the USA and Japan to China, southeast Asian countries (e.g. Vietnam, Indonesia) and the Philippines

### Key term

**Gini coefficient** A statistical measure used to assess the extent to which the distribution of income (income inequality) among the people of a country varies from a perfectly equal distribution.

### Exam tip

Be aware of the advantages and disadvantages of each of these indicators of social inequality.

### Key terms

**Gated communities** Wealthy residential areas that are fenced off and have security gates and entry systems.

**'Sink estates'** Social housing estates that are the least desirable to live in — they tend to house the lowest income, and most in need, residents.

**Global shift** The movement of manufacturing and some service industries from ACs to EDCS and LIDCs.

- service industries have also moved, especially to India, where back-office clerical and call-centre jobs have relocated
- ACs have responded by concentrating on specialist high-tech R&D and manufacturing, e.g. **science parks**

**Key term**

**Science park** An industrial and business zone focused on the quaternary industry and usually involving a university as a key partner.

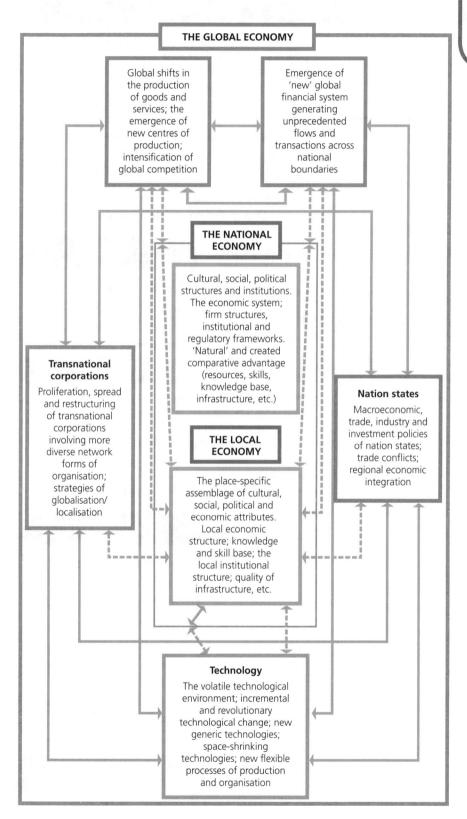

**Figure 14 Economic changes and the process of globalisation**

Table 15 shows the benefits and costs resulting from the global shift for the host countries.

**Table 15 Benefits and costs resulting from the global shift — host countries**

| Benefits | Costs |
|---|---|
| <ul><li>structural investments: roads, airports, ports, power stations</li><li>more formal employment with wages, and less informal employment</li><li>investment in education and skills for local people</li><li>reduced levels of inequality and poverty within the countries</li><li>governments gain income from increased levels of personal taxation — funds better public services</li><li>general public gain access to AC assets, e.g. the internet, tourism abroad</li></ul> | <ul><li>due to poor governance, some investments are poorly planned and located</li><li>rapid rural–urban migration leads to urban sprawl — again, often poorly planned</li><li>puts pressure on natural resources, e.g. water, energy supplies</li><li>sweatshop industries — very low wages and poor working conditions</li><li>the beginning of 'Westernisation' as local traditions decline</li><li>severe environmental issues: air pollution, groundwater pollution and deforestation</li></ul> |

Table 16 shows the benefits and costs resulting from the global shift for the source countries.

**Table 16 Benefits and costs resulting from the global shift — source countries**

**Exam tip**

Provide specific examples of some of these benefits and costs in identified places.

| Benefits | Costs |
|---|---|
| <ul><li>restructuring of industry — leading to changes in employment types</li><li>lower levels of industrial pollution — air and water</li><li>declining populations in some city regions — less pressure on services</li><li>investment in training and skills — a need to re-equip the workforce</li></ul> | <ul><li>de-industrialisation (Figure 15) on a large scale results in increasing unemployment</li><li>increasing levels of dereliction — abandoned factories and industrial wasteland, which may be contaminated</li><li>increase in poverty levels within urban areas</li><li>increase in urban unrest — with some forms of crime increasing (violence and theft)</li></ul> |

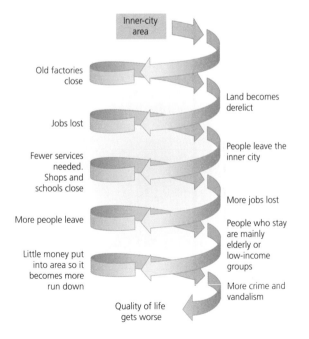

**Key terms**

**De-industrialisation** The closure of traditional manufacturing industries, e.g. steel, textiles.

**Restructuring** The change from one type of industry in an area to another — usually from manufacturing to service-based.

**Exam tip**

Provide specific examples of some of these benefits and costs in identified places.

**Figure 15 The spiral of decline from de-industrialisation**

# Booms and recessions

Key points:

- the economic status of a place is rarely static — there are periods of growth (booms) and periods of stagnation (recessions)
- such cyclical economic change has varied impacts on social opportunities and inequality
- during booms there is often technological innovation and new industrial development, creating opportunities for many
- these do not occur everywhere, however — rich core regions develop with poorer peripheral regions
- recessions impact places in different ways — more economically diversified and better educated places tend to be more resilient

Recently there has been a slowdown in the global shift:

- the financial crash of 2007/08 greatly impacted the global economy, and the effects of this are still being felt
- the Chinese economy is maturing and its growth rate has recently halved
- there are growing signs of opposition to globalisation

# The role of government

Governments can reduce or reinforce or create patterns of social inequality through their actions in spending or cutting key services such as education, healthcare, infrastructure and community services (Table 17).

Table 17 Examples of government action on social inequality

| Country type | Commentary |
| --- | --- |
| ACs | ■ spending on education, pensions and healthcare (e.g. the NHS) <br> ■ spending (or otherwise) on rural communication systems, including broadband |
| EDCs | ■ spending on infrastructural developments to support economic growth, e.g. ports and airports <br> ■ spending on improvements to healthcare facilities |
| LIDCs | ■ dependent on aid to combat diseases and famines <br> ■ trade deals with ACs and EDCs often involve much-needed social investment |

## Case studies: Social inequality

You are required to have **two** case studies of contrasting places that illustrate:

- evidence of **social inequality**
- the range of factors that influence social inequality
- how social inequality impacts people's daily lives in different ways

You should be able to describe evidence of social inequality for each place, such as:

- the quality of housing (e.g. detached, semi-detached, terraced, flats) and materials (e.g. brick, wood, corrugated iron sheets)
- the environmental quality of the place (e.g. air, water and land quality), how densely built-up the place is and the noise levels
- crime rates (e.g. using official statistics — see box below)
- the digital divide (e.g. access to telecommunications; availability and speed of digital connections)

You should be able to show how the level of social inequality is influenced by a range of factors, such as:

- demographic characteristics of the people living in the place (e.g. age, gender, ethnicity)
- social characteristics of the people (e.g. health levels; educational attainment)
- economic characteristics such as income, type of jobs (including factors such as full- or part-time), level of personal mobility (e.g. access to public transport or car-ownership level)

You should be able to relate the evidence of social inequality and factors influencing its level to the daily lives of the people living in each place.

## Exam tips

- These two case studies could be the same place(s) you studied in Section 3.1 What is a place? (page 41).
- For a UK-based case study, in addition to the online sources given on page 42, you could use the following for evidence of crime rates:
- http://crime-statistics.co.uk — data are from 2010; crimes are displayed within a 1-mile radius of a selected postcode
- www.police.uk — allows a comparison of the crime levels in different neighbourhoods
- http://maps.met.police.uk — allows users to see what offences (criminal and antisocial) have been reported in local streets

## Do you know?

1 Why is housing a good indicator of social inequality?

2 Distinguish between 'quality of life' and 'standard of living'.

3 Why is the concept of relative poverty useful when investigating social inequality?

4 Periods of boom and recession (bust) are said to go in cycles. What are these cycles called?

# 3.3 Players and placemaking processes

## You need to know

■ places are influenced by a range of players operating at different scales

■ places are produced in a variety of ways at different scales

■ rebranding is a placemaking process involving re-imaging and regeneration

■ making a successful place requires planning and design

## Players

Economic change in a place is driven by players (Table 18). The views of players depend on:

■ their own perceptions, lived experiences, attachments and motives

■ their use of different criteria to judge success or otherwise

■ the ability of leaders and planners to create places to attract an ever-more-mobile and educated population and customer base

■ party politics, which may affect decisions and the longevity of any scheme, e.g.:

  □ achieving 'good value for money'

  □ intervention is only necessary if market forces fail

  □ ensuring economic change is a local matter rather than a national priority

  □ the relative roles of public and private investment

### Key terms

**Players** Individuals, groups, organisations and stakeholders involved in any geographical issue of the decision-making process — they may be international, national and local governments or TNCs, pressure groups or any interested party.

**Criteria** Standards or measures used to make a judgement.

**Table 18 Players and their attitudes to economic change**

| Player | Attitude |
|---|---|
| International institution (e.g. the EU) | Willing to provide grants to support new infrastructure, e.g. new roads, railways or bridges (e.g. the European Regional Development Fund) |
| National government | Seek to fit economic change into a national strategy of regional development |
| Local government | Need to attract investment so as to raise living standards and reduce levels of deprivation |
| Businesses (TNCs or local) | Financial organisations (e.g. banks, pension-fund managers, insurance companies) seek a reward for their investments<br><br>TNCs and local businesses want an increase in trade, footfall and hence profits, and to be able to offer employment |
| Property developers | Seek to maximise profits through sales of houses and higher rental values |
| Non-governmental organisations (NGOs) | Often have an environmental focus, seeking to protect an environment (built or natural) from damage (e.g. National Trust, English Heritage) |
| Residents | Better housing; more employment opportunities; better community facilities; increased sense of well-being and belonging |

## Case study: Structural economic change

You are required to have **one** case study of a country or region that has been impacted by **structural economic change**.

Your case study must illustrate:

- the structural economic change that the country or region has gone through
- the role of players in driving the changes
- the impacts on places and people living in the country or region

You should be able to describe:

- the characteristics of the country or region before the economic change occurred, including demographic, socio-economic, cultural and environmental characteristics
- the economic changes that took place, e.g. from manufacturing to services or from agricultural to manufacturing
- the different players involved in driving the change, and their roles
- the impacts on the people living in the country or region of the economic change, including demographic, socio-economic, cultural and environmental impacts

## Exam tips

- Note: This case study **cannot** be one of the ones used previously — it has to be at a national or regional scale.
- Examples of suitable types of places are:
  - regions in ACs that have undergone de-industrialisation, e.g. parts of Lancashire and Yorkshire (UK), the Ruhr (Germany) or Detroit/Chicago (USA)
  - regions in ACs, EDCs or LIDCs that have undergone economic growth, e.g. Cambridge (UK), Bangalore (India), Pearl River Delta (China)
  - EDCs or LIDCs that have undergone economic change, such as industrialisation, e.g. Thailand or the Philippines

# Placemaking

## Governments and organisations

Key points:
- a number of large-scale players can affect a place profile — governments, TNCs and international/global institutions
- they often act together to change the character of a place, and so it is difficult to separate out their relative impacts:
  - □ governments: national governments invest in the infrastructure of a place, thereby enabling change; local authorities (LAs) give enticements to others to invest in the place
  - □ TNCs: provide investment that gives them the greatest return, e.g. a factory or a hotel complex
  - □ the EU: has provided vast sums of money to regenerate declining areas across the UK

> **Exam tip**
>
> Know some examples of where TNCs have provided FDI to stimulate economic change in a place. The TNCs may be based in either ACs or EDCs.

## Planners and architects

Key points:
- LAs compete to create attractive business environments for investors and highly skilled workers
- this may include housing, new roads, and even factories and offices for rent
- they develop local plans that designate specific areas for development, e.g. science parks for knowledge-based industries that are important for economic growth
- architects seek to enhance the built environment to make an area more attractive to investment
- waterfront developments with mixed uses, designated by planners and designed by architects, have become increasingly popular around the world

> **Exam tip**
>
> Know some examples of waterfront developments, e.g. Belfast's Titanic Quarter, London's Docklands, canalside areas in Birmingham, and similar developments in Cape Town and Vancouver.

The 24-hour city:
- many large urban areas are developing 24-hour rhythms, with constant but differing activities throughout the day (Figure 16)
- this is often a response to the targeted rebranding of a city for young adults, many of whom live in the city centre (see page 58)
- transport systems may run through the night, e.g. parts of the London Underground (Friday and Saturday only)
- some clubs, bars, fast-food outlets and services, e.g. gyms and supermarkets, are open late or all night
- refuse collection and shop deliveries are often scheduled to take place overnight, especially in pedestrianised areas

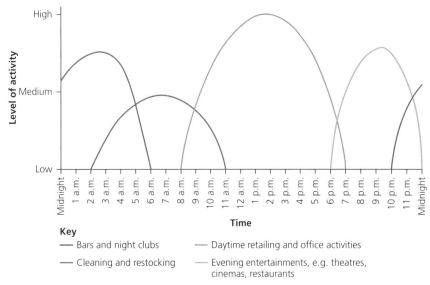

Figure 16 **Changes to an urban place through a 24-hour period**

# Local community groups

Key points:
- local interest groups, e.g. Chambers of Commerce, local preservation (heritage) societies and residents' associations, play varying roles in placemaking
- there are often tensions between groups that wish to preserve places and those that seek change
- they may be categorised by their viewpoint or stance: socio-economic, historical or environmental
- affluent areas tend to have more vociferous and mobilised local interest groups
- social media (e.g. Facebook, Twitter) allows people to create, share and exchange information, ideas, opinions and images and thereby to lobby local decision-makers

# Rebranding
## Strategies

Key points:
- the image (or brand) of a place is made up of objective features (e.g. site and situation) and subjective features (e.g. old or modern, clean or dirty, safe or unsafe)
- the authorities of many cities adopt a range of strategies to change this image through rebranding, re-imaging and ultimately regeneration (Figure 17 and Table 19)
- these processes can also take place in rural areas (Table 20)
- these strategies can be used singularly, or in conjunction with others to change the place meaning of a location

**Key terms**

Rebranding Changing the perceived image of a place for visitors and investors by marketing methods.

Re-imaging Using a variety of media to improve the perception of locations to make them more attractive to investors.

Regeneration The investment of capital and ideas into a rundown city area to revitalise it and renew its economic, social and/or environmental condition.

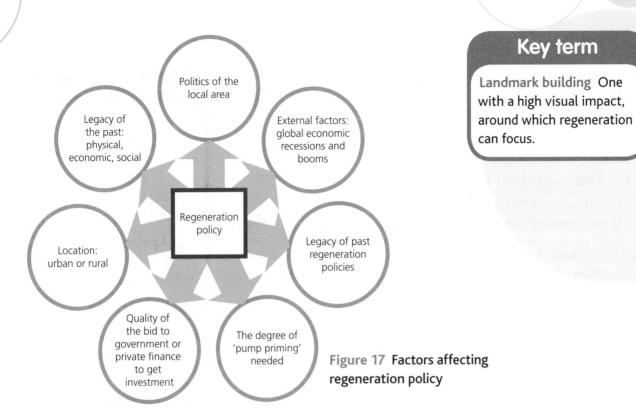

**Figure 17 Factors affecting regeneration policy**

Table 19 **Urban rebranding strategies**

| Strategy | Commentary and examples |
|---|---|
| Retail-led | ■ major shopping centres, e.g. Westfield sites (London, Derby, Bradford); Trafford Centre (Manchester)<br>■ street markets, e.g. Christmas markets<br>■ shopping combined with other features, e.g. malls in Dubai |
| Heritage-led | ■ historic sites making use of landmark buildings, e.g. Belfast's Titanic Quarter<br>■ castle sites, e.g. Warwick and Cardiff Castles<br>■ architectural sites, e.g. Covent Garden and central Birmingham |
| Sport-led | ■ London Olympics and Paralympics (the London Stadium)<br>■ Sports City, Manchester (the Velodrome and Etihad Stadium)<br>■ the Millennium Stadium, Cardiff |
| Art and culture-led | ■ re-working of old buildings, e.g. Sage, Gateshead<br>■ European Capital of Culture, e.g. Hull, Liverpool<br>■ media-influenced, Media City and Lowry Theatre, Salford<br>■ artwork by Banksy, Bristol |
| Food-led | ■ various Chinatowns in cities, e.g. London and Manchester<br>■ specialist foods, e.g. the Cittaslow movement in Ludlow |

Table 20 **Rural rebranding strategies**

| Strategy | Commentary and examples |
|---|---|
| Leisure-led | ■ custom-built private facilities, e.g. Center Parcs |
| Sport-led | ■ outdoor activities in forest parks, e.g. Galloway (Scotland) and Thetford (Norfolk)<br>■ outdoor activities in old quarries, e.g. Zip World and Bounce Below in Blaenau Ffestiniog (north Wales) |
| Art and culture-led | ■ connections with famous authors/poets, e.g. Thomas Hardy (Dorset); Brontë Country (Yorkshire); Wordsworth (Grasmere)<br>■ media connections, e.g. *Downton Abbey* (Highclere Castle, Hampshire and Bampton, Oxfordshire); *Broadchurch* (Dorset); Harry Potter (Alnwick Castle)<br>■ heritage-based, e.g. Northumberland coast with castles, fishing harbours and religious links — Holy Island |

# Contests

Groups of people can contest efforts to rebrand a place, due to:
- different views about the priorities and strategies for rebranding/regeneration
- a lack of political engagement and representation — **marginalised people**
- **social polarisation** and a lack of economic opportunity for some
- in rural areas, **NIMBY** groups protest over planned developments, e.g. new housing areas, wind farms and proposed fracking sites

Figure 18 shows some of the contested aspects associated with the regeneration of the east London area for the 2012 London Olympics.

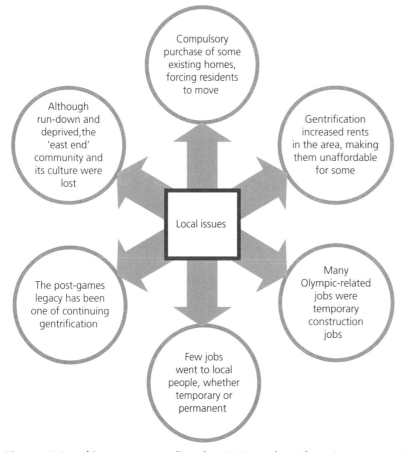

Figure 18 Local issues surrounding the 2012 London Olympics regeneration

## Case study: Rebranding

You are required to have **one** case study of a place (either urban or rural) that has undergone **rebranding**.

Your case study must illustrate:
- why the place needed to rebrand
- the strategy/strategies involved in the rebranding
- the role and influence of the range of players involved in the placemaking process
- how the rebranding altered people's perceptions of the place
- an evaluation of the relative success of the rebranding

You should describe the following:

- characteristics of the place before rebranding occurred, to include demographic, socio-economic, cultural and environmental characteristics — you should include a summary of what the overall perception of the place was before rebranding
- the strategy/strategies used in the rebranding process, such as economic restructuring from primary activities (e.g. farming and forestry) and/or manufacturing to services (e.g. tourism, retail or office-based employment), the use of architecture, the use of heritage and/or sporting and/or cultural events
- the different players involved in driving the rebranding including their roles, e.g. national and/or local government, TNCs and/ or international institutions (e.g. EU, non-governmental organisations, local community groups)
- how the perception of the place has been altered as a result of the rebranding process

You should offer an assessment of the extent to which the rebranding has achieved its aim, including an evaluation of how different players view the results of the rebranding, such as whether they think that their lives and/or the place are improved as a result of the rebranding.

## Exam tips

- This case study could be one of the places you studied in Section 3.1 What is a place? (page 41).
- Possible examples of a **UK urban area** are Salford Quays (Manchester), the Olympic Park (Stratford, east London), Doncaster Earth Centre (Doncaster), Broad Street (Birmingham), Coin Street (London) and the new Chinatown (Liverpool).
- Possible examples of a **UK rural area** could be the North Antrim coast (Northern Ireland), Balmedie (Aberdeenshire), Croyde (Devon) and Hebden Bridge (West Yorkshire).

## End of section 3 questions

1 Explain the types of evidence that could be used to show social inequality.

2 Explain why different urban communities may have contrasting views about regeneration.

3 For a local place you have studied, explain why people's sense of identity has been influenced by the economic and social change it has experienced.

4 Evaluate the importance of rebranding to the success of rural regeneration.

5 Assess the extent to which economic regeneration brings benefits to rural areas.

6 Explain how globalisation can influence people's sense of place.

7 How can a place be seen to develop in layers of time?

8 Assess the extent to which the experiences of people living in an urban place that you have studied have been affected by the development of the area's infrastructure.

9 'Community groups are the most important players in the placemaking process.' To what extent do you agree with this statement?

10 'Placemaking is used by governments only to attract inward investment.' To what extent do you agree with this statement?

## Do you know?

1 Where are most of the UK's science parks situated?

2 What is meant by the '24-hour city'?

3 Give one advantage and one disadvantage of using social media when investigating attitudes to placemaking processes.

4 Describe the regeneration of one urban area you have studied.

5 Outline one set of contested views regarding a rebranding process.

# 4 Global connections options

## Global systems: Option B — Global migration

## 4.1 Contemporary patterns

### You need to know

- migration involves dynamic flows of people between countries, regions and continents
- current patterns of international migration are related to global patterns of socio-economic development

## Flows

### Patterns

Key points:

- in 2015 it was estimated that more than 240 million people (over 3% of global population) lived in a country they were not born in
- modern transport networks enable global labour flows to operate
- changes to living conditions, such as mechanisation and land-grabs, cause people to move internally, e.g. from rural China to coastal cities such as Shenzhen
- much international migration is intra-regional, e.g. the USA to Mexico, or within the EU following the Schengen Agreement (Table 21)

Table 21 Current inter-regional and intra-regional migration patterns and general factors causing them

| Area of origin | Area of destination | Reasons for movement |
| --- | --- | --- |
| South Asia/ southeast Asia | West Asia (Middle East) | Economic — migrants with low skills, seeking relatively low wages (though high for them) |
| South Asia | Europe | Family reunification |
| South Asia | North America | Economic — migrants with high skills, seeking high wages |

### Key terms

**International migration** Takes place between countries, for a minimum of 1 year.

**Migration** A permanent or semi-permanent change of residence.

**Economic migrant** A person who moves voluntarily for work or to improve his/her social conditions.

| Area of origin | Area of destination | Reasons for movement |
|---|---|---|
| South Asia | South Asia | Intra-regional economic movement from poorer countries to relatively richer countries in the same region (e.g. Myanmar to Thailand) |
| Latin America | Europe | Strong cultural ties |
| North America | Europe | Economic — migrants with high skills, seeking high wages; linked to TNC growth |
| Sub-Saharan Africa and western Asia | Europe | Economic — migrants with low skills, seeking low wages; refugees and asylum seekers |
| Europe | Europe | Intra-regional economic migrants with low skills from east Europe to west Europe; return economic migration of higher-skilled to country of origin |

## Numbers

Figure 19 illustrates the numbers involved for some of the world's largest receivers of international migrants, and how they have changed over recent years.

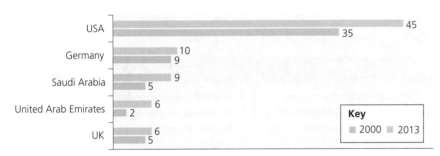

**Figure 19** Number of international migrants living in selected countries (2000 and 2013) — millions

In the UK in 2015:

- 6.5 million people were foreign-born
- the three largest 'sending' countries were India, Poland and Pakistan
- most migrants were economic migrants, with others being either students or seeking family reunification

# Development and inequality
## National indices

Migrant **remittances**:

- have increased by four times since 2000
- amounted to over $400 billion per year (2015) being sent from ACs to EDCs and LIDCs

- some suggest the amount is larger, as the above is just the recorded flow of money — cash amounts are unknown
- reduce the level of poverty in the 'home' country — they allow money to be spent on health, education, housing and establishing small businesses
- can stimulate an economic multiplier effect by creating local employment opportunities
- help to reduce the incidence of child labour in the receiving countries

HDI (see page 48):
- note: there is a strong inverse relationship between receipt of migrant remittances and HDI:
  - □ ACs tend to receive amounts of migrant remittances that are only a low percentage of GDP
  - □ for LIDCs and EDCs, migrant remittances are a much higher percentage of GDP

> ### Key term
>
> GDP Gross Domestic Product.

# Stability, growth and development

Table 22 shows the impact of migration on stability, economic growth and development.

Table 22 **Impact of migration on stability, economic growth and development**

| Stability | Economic growth | Development |
|---|---|---|
| ■ remittances act as a source of foreign exchange, providing economic stability<br>■ returning migrants bring new ideas and values to the home country, e.g. democracy and equality, providing social stability<br>■ youthful migrants can balance an ageing population, providing demographic stability | ■ the tax base in the receiving country is increased by working migrants, thereby raising national GDP<br>■ consumer spending is increased by working migrants, stimulating local economies<br>■ migrants often 'fill' labour shortages, in skilled and unskilled occupations<br>■ remittances can stimulate growth (multiplier effect) in the 'home' country | ■ the skills and knowledge acquired by returning migrants benefit families, local communities and the country as a whole<br>■ social networks are often created, leading to further flows of money, skills and professional expertise<br>■ international organisations (e.g. the UN) can establish development projects between receiving and donor countries to support migration networks<br>■ 'bottom-up' projects can be financed by remittances |

# Inequality, conflict and injustices

Table 23 shows the impact of migration on inequality, conflict and injustices.

> ### Exam tip
>
> Be able to provide specific examples of some of these impacts arising from migration.

Table 23 Impact of migration on inequality, conflict and injustices

| Inequality | Conflict | Injustice |
|---|---|---|
| ■ donor countries lose large numbers of their young and aspirant population<br>■ it is often the more educated who leave, so skill levels drop<br>■ birth rates fall in the donor countries<br>■ some families receive more remittances than others, creating inequality within communities | ■ in the receiving country there may be disagreements between host communities and migrants<br>■ there are often increasing pressures placed on social services — health and education<br>■ borders require control of illegal migrants and human traffickers<br>■ the rise of right-wing political parties causes discontent | ■ migrants are vulnerable to violation of their human rights — forced labour, human trafficking<br>■ asylum seekers are held in detention centres, unable to work though being supported<br>■ the number of refugees is rising, with issues regarding shelter, food, water and safety becoming more prevalent<br>■ deportation numbers are also increasing |

## Do you know?

1 What is the Schengen Agreement?
2 Outline one major refugee migration that you have studied.
3 Where are the major sources of refugees today?
4 Identify one area where migration has been of ethnically similar but culturally different people.
5 Why are migrant remittances important in the development process?

## Exam tips

■ Be able to provide specific examples of some of these issues arising from migration.
■ Note the key role played by technology — it is used both to monitor migration patterns and to assist in crisis management.

# 4.2 Complexities

## You need to know

■ migration patterns are influenced by a multitude of interrelated factors
■ corridors of migrant flows create interdependence between countries

# Factors

## Economic globalisation

General points:

■ globalisation has caused significant changes in the global economic system
■ there are disparities of wealth between different areas of the world, causing people to want to better their lives and find work
■ this has led to a rise in migration, both internal and international
■ new countries of origin and destination have emerged during the twenty-first century (see Table 21, page 62)

## Key term

**Internal migration** Takes place within a country, e.g. rural to urban migration.

- internal migration has taken place on a massive scale in China, India, Brazil, Indonesia and Mexico, caused by the employment opportunities created by FDI

# Age and gender

Key points:
- the majority of economic migrants are young adults, between 25 and 39 years
- the majority of these migrants are male — population structures often have a gender imbalance in this age range as a result
- female migration is increasing — either low-skilled in domestic work, e.g. in the Gulf, or high-skilled in finance and business, e.g. in the UK and USA

# South–South corridors

It is believed that migrant flows between countries in the 'South' are now equal to those between the 'South' and the 'North'.

Reasons for this include:
- restrictions — some states (e.g. Australia, the USA) attempt to control flows of migration
- rapid economic growth is taking place in some countries in the 'South'
- the high costs of movements to the 'North'
- trade associations in the 'South', e.g. ASEAN and Mercosur, enabling migration
- technology (e.g. wire transfer) enabling the easier sending of remittances
- an increase in refugees from countries in the 'South' to near neighbours

# Refugees

Key points:
- in 2015 the UNHCR estimated that there were over 17 million refugees worldwide
- historically, countries affected by civil war or by persecution of minority groups on the grounds of religion or ethnicity, or governed by political regimes that punished dissent, have all produced large refugee populations
- economic hardship, combined with persecution from forced labour and modern-day slavery, has also created refugees, as have natural hazards and climate change
- IDPs are refugees within their own country, and are often not officially recorded

## Key terms

'South' A generic term for the less developed areas of the world, many of which are in the southern hemisphere.

'North' A generic term for the developed areas of the world, many of which are in the northern hemisphere.

ASEAN The Association of Southeast Asian Nations.

Mercosur An economic grouping of Argentina, Brazil, Paraguay and Uruguay.

## Exam tip

Note the terms 'North' and 'South' are not used very often today as they are regarded as being too simplistic — the OCR specification uses them here despite using other notations for countries elsewhere.

## Key terms

UNHCR United Nations High Commission for Refugees.

IDPs Internally displaced persons.

# Policies

Key points:

- globalisation has created an ease of communication that allows aspirant and oppressed people to be aware of a better world
- some countries (e.g. Canada) have encouraged immigration to fill labour shortages, and other countries (e.g. Pakistan) have encourage emigration to gain the financial benefits from remittances
- security fears and a widespread reluctance to help migrants and refugees, however, have fuelled a spate of new immigration policies and controls
- those with capital and a valuable skill will always find it relatively easy to migrate
- those without both, and who are desperate to move due to prejudice or oppression, find it more challenging — the ILO has been established to assist these people (Figure 20)
- a number of controls have been set up to manage migration (Table 24)

## Key term

**ILO** International Labour Organization — an agency of the UN.

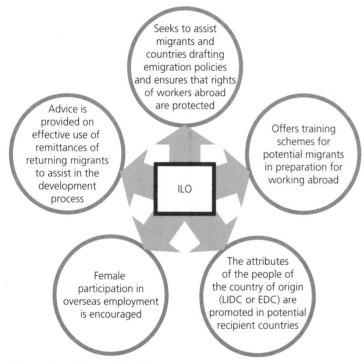

**Figure 20  The work of the ILO**

Table 24 Examples of controls on international migration

| Country | Commentary |
|---|---|
| USA | 'Open door' policy in the early twentieth century, followed by Green Card system; currently strong immigration controls (fingerprinting and retina photographs) and deportation; proposal to build a wall on Mexican/USA border |
| Australia | Before 1973, a racial/ethnic selection process called 'White Australia'; currently a points-based system for economic migrants; refugees are held on small offshore islands |
| Canada | Points-based system — needs to attract high-skilled workers, e.g. engineers and health workers |
| Schengen Europe | Free movement of people across borders — no controls |

## Bilateral flows

Distinct corridors of bilateral flows (migrant flows between two countries) have developed:

- Mexico to the USA — although in 2018 President Trump is seeking to reduce this
- Palestine to Jordan — movements of refugees
- Myanmar to Thailand — economic movement
- India/Bangladesh to the UAE — economic movement
- Poland to the UK — economic movement

Reasons for such flows may include one or more of the following:

- ease and low cost of travel
- ability to send home remittances
- employment opportunities
- strong support networks within communities
- legacy of former colonial connections and/or similar language

## Corridors of migrant flows

Key points:

- international migration illustrates interdependence between countries
- socio-economic interdependence can occur where economic migrants provide labour in a receiving country and on their return bring newly acquired skills, ideas and values to their home country
- economic interdependence can occur through trade, when an AC exports manufactured goods to an EDC or LIDC and imports raw materials in return

### Key terms

Colonial The establishment and maintenance of rule by a sovereign power over the people of an empire — it was a feature of the nineteenth and early twentieth centuries, with several European countries having colonies.

Interdependence The mutual dependence of two or more countries, between which there is a reciprocal relationship.

### Exam tip

Try to keep up to date with this contemporary topic.

## Case study: Interdependence

You are required to have **one** case study of an **EDC to illustrate interdependence**.

For your chosen case study, you should illustrate the following:

- current patterns of immigration and emigration, possibly including statistics for the flows
- changes in immigration and emigration over time — this could include both recent changes, e.g. the effects of trading bloc membership on flows, and also historic flows, perhaps linked to the colonial period, and their legacy
- examples of economic, social, political and environmental interdependence, with countries connected to the EDC by migrant flows:
  - relationships with bilateral migration partners
  - economic interdependence, e.g. employment opportunities and remittances
  - socio-economic interdependence, e.g. development of support mechanisms
  - political interdependence, e.g. trade agreements and sharing of security issues
  - environmental interdependence, e.g. cooperation in dealing with pollution or the protection of ecosystems
- the impact of migration on the country's economic development, political stability and social equality — to include both opportunities and challenges at different scales

### Exam tip

Examples of EDCs include India, Brazil or Bangladesh. You could also consider studying small island states such as Jamaica, Martinique and Samoa/Tonga.

## Do you know?

1 What are IDPs?

2 In what way is an asylum seeker different from a refugee?

3 Outline the impact of colonialism on one country.

# 4.3 Associated issues

## You need to know

- migration creates opportunities and challenges that reflect the unequal power relations between countries

# Case studies

For this part of the specification you are required to have studied **two** case studies to illustrate how:

■ **ACs** have the power to influence and drive change
■ **LIDCs** have limited power and influence to drive change

The impact of these unequal power relations on people and places in terms of opportunities and challenges in the context of migration should be examined.

## Case study: Advanced countries

For your chosen AC, include the following:

■ patterns of immigration and emigration — the main countries of origin of immigrants, the reasons for the attractiveness of the AC for immigrant populations, the main destination countries for emigrants from the AC and the reasons for emigration
■ details of the AC's migration policies and their rationale
■ an understanding of the interdependence of the AC with countries linked to it by international migration — this could include the economic, social, political and environmental relationships developed by the AC in its bilateral migration corridors
■ opportunities and challenges created within the AC as a result of international migration

Opportunities could include:

■ addressing labour shortages in both low-skilled and highly skilled jobs in different sectors of industry
■ stimulating local multiplier effects and demographic effects, e.g. the impact of increased birth rate on the population structure of the AC

Challenges could include:

■ the problems for border control in dealing with unauthorised immigrants
■ people trafficking, contraband and security
■ the integration of immigrant populations into the society of the host AC
■ the supply of services and resources where immigrant populations are concentrated

### Exam tip

Examples of ACs include the UK, France, Germany, Australia and the USA.

## Case study: Low-income developing countries

For your chosen LIDC, include the following:

- patterns of emigration and immigration — the main destination countries for emigrants from the LIDC, the reasons for emigration, the main countries of origin for immigrants to the LIDC and the reasons for immigration
- details of the LIDC's migration policies and their rationale, together with any additional laws on migration to which the LIDC is subject as a member of a trading bloc
- an understanding of the interdependence of the LIDC with countries linked to it by international migration — this could include the economic, social, political and environmental relationships developed by the LIDC in its bilateral migration corridors
- opportunities and challenges created within the LIDC as a result of international migration

Opportunities could include:

- stimulation of political and economic cooperation with other countries, especially where bilateral links are strengthening
- the specific benefits of migrant remittances at different scales, and increasing political stability

Challenges could include:

- the effects of the 'brain drain', including loss of low-skilled and highly skilled labour
- problems of exploitation of workers by human trafficking, forced labour and exploitation

### Exam tip

Examples of LIDCs include Bangladesh, Haiti, Ethiopia, Niger and Zimbabwe.

## Do you know?

1 What is meant by 'socio-economic interdependence'?

2 Identify some challenges for LIDCs presented by international migration.

## End of option B questions

1 Describe the rural to urban migration that has taken place in one country you have studied.

2 Suggest ways in which the number of immigrants living in an area can influence flows of money.

3 Discuss the varying implications of international migration for both countries of origin and destination countries.

4 With reference to a case study, explain how emigration from a low-income developing country can provide opportunities for that LIDC.

5 Assess the factors that might account for the spatial variation in refugees and asylum seekers.

# Global governance: Option D — Power and borders

# 4.4 Sovereignty and territorial integrity

## You need to know
- the world political map of sovereign nation states is dynamic
- a multitude of factors pose challenges to sovereignty and territorial integrity

## Nation states

### Definitions

Key points:
- national **states** vary greatly in their ethnic, cultural and linguistic unity
- a state may have several **nations** within it, e.g. the UK with England, Scotland, Wales and Northern Ireland
- a state may also have other varied characteristics, e.g. different faiths, different dialects
- some states have evolved with a widely varied mix of peoples, e.g. the USA (sometimes described as a 'melting pot') and Singapore
- some states have evolved with a narrow range of characteristics and have a homogeneous culture, e.g. Iceland
- factors influencing such characteristics include the history of population growth (particularly migration over time) and relative physical and political isolation
- states have internationally defined and agreed legal rights of **sovereignty** and **territorial integrity**
- according to Article 2.4 of the UN Charter, member states must not use force or threaten the territorial integrity or sovereignty of another state

### The world political map

Key points:
- the world political map shows the boundaries and territories of sovereign states

### Key terms

**State**  A territory over which no other country holds power or sovereignty.

**Nation**  A group of people with a common identity, who may, or may not, have sovereignty.

**Sovereignty**  The absolute power exercised by governments of states over their land and people.

**Territorial integrity**  The principle that the defined territory of a state, over which it has exclusive and legitimate control, is inviolable.

### Exam tip

Check the locations of the areas in Figure 21 in an atlas or online, e.g. using Google Maps or Bing Maps.

■ changes to borders and the formation of new countries illustrate that the world political map is dynamic (Figure 21)

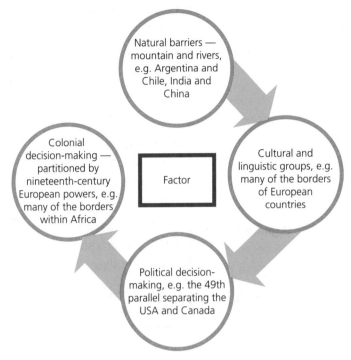

**Figure 21 Factors influencing national borders**

# Norms

Key points:
■ the United Nations (UN) has created a number of long-established **norms**
■ it includes 193 countries as its Member States, and its main headquarters is located in New York, USA

The UN:
■ states that only through international cooperation can mankind meet the challenges facing the world
■ operates through applying the principles of its Charter, which treats nation states as equal partners
■ maintains international peace and stability via the Security Council, which has some permanent members (the USA, China, Russia, the UK) and others in rotation
■ does not maintain its own military — its peacekeeping forces are supplied by member states
■ aims to protect human rights by adopting the **UDHR** as a standard
■ applies economic or diplomatic sanctions to countries, in order to make them change their behaviour
■ upholds international law through the **ICJ** and a number of international treaties

## Key terms

**Norms** Moral principles, customs and ways of living that are universally accepted.

**UDHR** Universal Declaration of Human Rights.

**ICJ** International Court of Justice.

- in both 2000 and 2015, set targets (MDGs and SDGs, respectively) regarding tackling poverty, child and maternal mortality, diseases and environmental concerns
- established the IPCC, a scientific advisory panel, to inform debate on climate change and brief global conferences, e.g. the Kyoto Protocol (1997) and COP21 Paris (2015)

# Intervention

Intervention is controversial as it challenges the concepts of sovereignty and territorial integrity. It can consist of:

- economic sanctions, e.g. a trade embargo
- military action authorised by the UN
- peacekeeping missions by the UN and other regional organisations such as NATO
- humanitarian assistance by NGOs during crises (Figure 22)

Figure 22 Different roles of NGOs

Intervention may be deemed necessary when:

- there are human rights violations within a country
- there is aggression by one state against another
- civil war has erupted in a country
- terrorist activities originate from, and/or their perpetrators are being sheltered by, certain states

# Geopolitics

Geopolitics has created a classification of countries that are used throughout this specification:

- **Advanced countries (ACs)** — e.g. the USA and Germany, which have wealth, high levels of development and politically strong governments; they are in a strong position to drive and control global systems such as international trade and international migration
- **Emerging and developing countries (EDCs)** — e.g. China, India and Brazil, which are increasingly powerful economically and politically

■ **Low-income developing countries (LIDCs)** — e.g. Sierra Leone and Bangladesh, which are much less powerful, have limited access to global markets and limited control over international migration

# Factors and challenges

In the globalised world of the twenty-first century, the concepts of sovereignty and territorial integrity are increasingly being challenged and eroded.

## Current political boundaries

Not all borders are recognised, and some are subject to dispute (Table 25).

**Table 25 Disputed borders**

| Border | Commentary on disputed aspects |
|---|---|
| Alsace/Lorraine | An area between France and Germany — rich in coal and iron ore, it has 'changed hands' several times |
| Russia/Ukraine/Crimea | The latter is important for Russia as a sea access to the Black Sea |
| Western Asia (Turkey/Iraq/Iran/Syria) | The desire for an autonomous Kurdish state |
| North/South Korea | The outcome of a fragile truce following the Korean War |
| Kashmir | Claimed by both India and Pakistan |
| The former Yugoslavia | A number of states were created when it broke up — the legitimacy of Kosovo is currently subject to discussion |
| South China Sea | Some maritime borders where rights over natural resources and exploration are contested between China, Vietnam and other countries |
| Taiwan | Not recognised by China, but recognised by the USA |

Nationalist movements in Europe:
■ strong nationalist movements have arisen, seeking to establish independent, smaller states — **separatism**
■ the causes may be due to different languages and cultures, a geographically peripheral location, an alienation from the central government, or a combination of these
■ examples in Europe include Catalonia, Scotland and Brittany
■ most European separatist groups seek to remain within the regional political union — the EU

> ## Exam tip
>
> Check the locations of these areas in an atlas or online, e.g. using Google Maps or Bing Maps.

> ## Key term
>
> **Separatism** A desire to have autonomy within, or independence from, a country.

> ## Exam tip
>
> This is a very contemporary topic — keep up to date.

# Transnational corporations

Transnational corporations (TNCs):

- dominate international trade — they are important drivers of the global economy
- can be either publicly owned (by shareholders) or state-led (by governments)
- occur in a wide range of industries — resource extraction (oil, metal ores), manufacturing (electronics, food, cars) and services (banking, supermarkets, hotels)
- are responsible for developing global supply chains through FDI in factories and businesses in EDCs, e.g. China and India
- have made further investments in sub-Saharan Africa, southeast Asia and Latin America
- invest heavily in new technologies and patents, which allows them to operate efficiently and make more money through royalties and licensing

Spatial organisation:

- most TNCs have headquarters and R&D in ACs
- manufacturing is usually based in areas of low labour costs — southeast Asia and eastern Europe

Production:

- most TNCs take advantage of outsourcing their production — some subcontracting arrangements can be highly complex
- many TNCs also outsource their back-office and other services

Impact on sovereignty:

- some LIDCs have become dependent on the economic and social benefits from TNC investment
- some argue that these countries have lost control of their sovereignty to TNCs
- low wage economies, poor working conditions and human rights abuses are blamed on TNCs
- the UN has sponsored schemes of corporate social responsibility — to protect and benefit employees and communities in areas with TNC involvement

# Supranational institutions

Key points:

- supranational institutions, e.g. NATO and the EU, represent a tier of governance above that of the individual state
- member states retain their sovereignty, including their independence, territorial integrity and responsibility for their citizens

## Key terms

TNCs Transnational corporations — companies that operate in more than one country (also known as multinationals).

Patent The legal protection given to a new invention.

Outsourcing A TNC subcontracts an 'overseas' company to produce goods or services on its behalf.

Corporate social responsibility A TNC's commitment to assess and take responsibility for its social and environmental impact — including its ethical behaviour towards the quality of life of its workforce, their families and local communities.

## Exam tip

Research a TNC that you can easily access information on, and that interests you. Examples include Apple, Ford, Shell and Tata.

- states are also bound by the requirements of the supranational body, however, including any treaties it signs
- some argue this is a partial 'surrender' of sovereignty

Military alliances:
- see Table 26

**Exam tip**

Russia also has a similar military agreement (Collective Security Treaty Organization) with most of its former USSR republics.

Table 26 **Supranational military alliances**

| Organisation | Commentary |
|---|---|
| NATO | - comprises the USA, Canada, Turkey and 25 European countries<br>- the main principle is that if one member is threatened, all others will come to its aid<br>- also promotes democratic values |
| ANZUS | - similar to NATO, but with trans-Pacific security in mind |

Regional trading blocs:
- see Figure 23 and Table 27

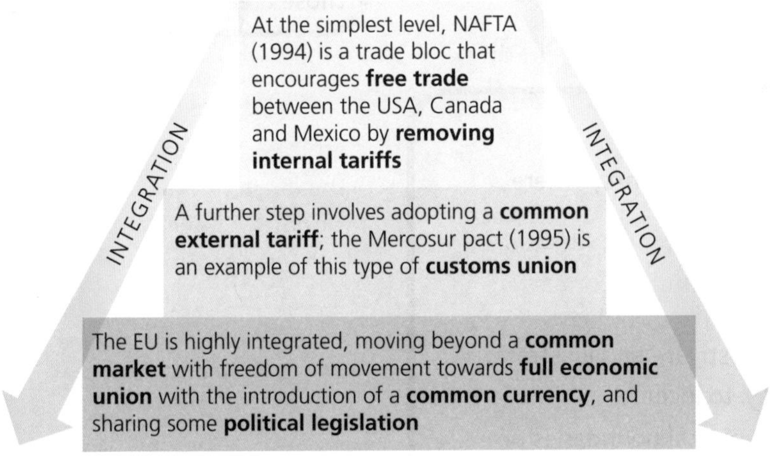

Figure 23 **Different types of trading blocs**

At the simplest level, NAFTA (1994) is a trade bloc that encourages **free trade** between the USA, Canada and Mexico by **removing internal tariffs**

A further step involves adopting a **common external tariff**; the Mercosur pact (1995) is an example of this type of **customs union**

The EU is highly integrated, moving beyond a **common market** with freedom of movement towards **full economic union** with the introduction of a **common currency**, and sharing some **political legislation**

INTEGRATION

**Key terms**

**ANZUS** The Australia, New Zealand and United States Security Treaty.

**Maquiladora** Manufacturing industries operating in a Mexican free trade zone close to the USA/Mexico border, where factories import materials and equipment on a duty-free and tariff-free basis for assembly, processing or manufacturing. The products are then re-exported back to the USA and Canada.

**Off-shoring** The manufacture or assembly of a product in a developing country using components produced in a developed country.

Table 27 **Economic alliances**

| Organisation | Commentary |
|---|---|
| EU | Consists of 28 member states (2018). There is ongoing debate about its success:<br>- **for**: with a huge potential market of around 500 million people, the combined strength of the members forms a powerful trade bloc; freedom of movement for workers within a wide employment market<br>- **against**: poor distribution of EU income, particularly as the Common Agricultural Policy (CAP) takes so much of the budget; over-bureaucracy within the European Commission has brought into question its efficiency; the adoption of some European law has been inconsistent across the Union |
| NAFTA | Members consist of the USA, Canada and Mexico; its main impact has been to create the maquiladora in Mexico, which is off-shoring based entirely on numerous low-cost labour forces in northern Mexico |
| ASEAN | A political and economic organisation of ten southeast Asian countries — Indonesia, Malaysia, the Philippines, Singapore, Thailand, Brunei, Cambodia, Laos, Myanmar and Vietnam; its aims include accelerating economic growth and social progress, and promoting regional peace and stability |

# Political dominance of ethnic groups

Key points:

- some borders, e.g. several within Africa, are the result of colonial decision-making — partitioned by nineteenth-century European powers
- colonial powers were concerned with dividing up Africa's raw materials and water resources among themselves
- by 1900, many African ethnic groups were living in newly formed nations that in no way represented their own heritage
- some long-established ethnic regions were split into two or more parts, with each becoming part of a different newly established nation state with problems of sovereignty and legitimacy
- this situation of ethnic groups spread across political boundaries also exists elsewhere, e.g. the Basques (Spain and France) and the Kurds (Turkey, Iraq and Syria)
- internal conflict may break out when there is an imbalance of ethnicities of some states, e.g. Rwanda and the Hutu/Tutsi peoples in the 1990s

> ### Exam tip
>
> Check the location of some African nation borders in an atlas or online, e.g. using Google Maps or Bing Maps, against the ethnicities in those areas.

## Case study: Sovereignty

You are required to have **one** case study of any country where **sovereignty has been challenged** to illustrate:

- causes and challenges to the government
- impacts on people and places

For your chosen case study you should investigate and illustrate:

a **Causes** of the challenge to sovereignty, to include:
  - political factors such as contested political boundaries or political dominance of ethnic groups seeking independence
  - economic factors such as the impacts of TNCs or the effects of membership of an economic/political union such as the EU
  - factors such as the cultural and political diversity, and the contribution of the country's physical, social and economic geography to this diversity

b **Challenges** to the government, to include:
  - 'threats from within', such as violence or protest in claiming separatism, and ethnic conflict
  - 'external threats' to territorial integrity, such as invasion or conflict over disputed boundaries or resources with a neighbouring state
  - the fragility of internal governance that has led to criminal activity, corruption or an electoral system that is unfair or unreliable

c **Impacts** on people and places, to include:
  - military activity leading to displacement of population, deaths and injuries

- damage to housing, poor access to services, medicines and food
- the effects of terrorism
- disruption to the economy, livelihoods and communications, and loss of power and energy supplies

## Exam tip

Examples could include Ukraine, South Sudan, Mali and Spain (Basques and Catalonia).

## Do you know?

1 Illustrate the dynamic nature of the world political map.
2 Which nationalities have created the 'melting pot' of the USA?
3 Give one example of a nation that does not have sovereignty.
4 What is meant by 'self-determination'?
5 What is the UN Global Compact?

# 4.5 Global governance

## You need to know

- global governance provides a framework to regulate conflict
- global governance involves cooperation between organisations at a variety of scales
- global governance of sovereignty and territorial integrity has consequences for people and places

# Frameworks

Global governance:

- has shaped the relationships between nation states and non-state organisations (e.g. the UN and NGOs)
- created the laws and institutions that have been responsible for positive changes in the way in which global geopolitics operates
- has dealt with matters such as those concerning trade, security, nuclear proliferation, human rights, sovereignty and territorial integrity, the atmosphere, laws of the sea and the protection of animals

Challenges to sovereignty and territorial integrity that cause conflict include:

- unjust treatment of citizens, e.g. restrictions in democratic elections
- competition for access to natural resources, e.g. trans-boundary water issues
- suppression or marginalisation of people seeking independence or autonomy

## Key terms

**Global governance** The emergence of norms, rules, laws and institutions that have regulated and reproduced the trade-orientated global systems, as well as other global systems (e.g. those involving patterns of population migration).

**Human rights** Moral principles or norms that describe certain standards of human behaviour. Protected as legal rights under international law.

- a government failing to ensure basic human needs, such as healthcare, hygiene, education and food, or to protect its citizens from violation of human rights
- persecution of people for their religious or political beliefs
- ethnic conflict within a state

# Institutions, treaties, laws and norms

The United Nations (in addition to material given on page 73):

- the UN was the first post-war IGO to be established and its role has grown in importance (Figure 24)
- its role in global governance is affected by the different geopolitical visions of the members of the Security Council
- it seeks to manage global environmental, socio-economic and political problems:
  - ☐ the UDHR defines global human rights in considerable detail
  - ☐ the UN Convention on the Rights of the Child (CRC)
  - ☐ the UNHCR supports people affected by conflict
  - ☐ the MDGs and their successor, the SDGs
  - ☐ the UN established the Geneva Convention, which protects the rights of prisoners

> **Key term**
>
> IGO Inter-governmental organisation.

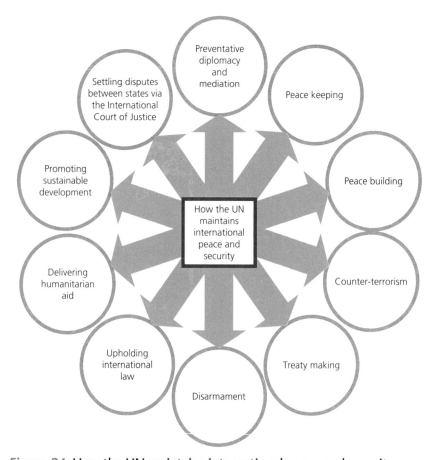

**Figure 24 How the UN maintains international peace and security**

Human rights:
- see Table 28

Table 28 UN actions to protect human rights

| Action | Nature and evaluation |
|---|---|
| Sanctions | - economic sanctions — restrictions on trade (e.g. against Iran)<br>- cultural sanctions — influencing sporting exchanges<br>- both designed to bring about change in human rights in targeted country; success has been limited |
| War crimes trials | - International Criminal Court established at The Hague (Netherlands) for crimes such as genocide<br>- trials are very slow — e.g. that of Radovan Karadžić (Bosnian Serb leader) lasted 8 years |
| UN troops | - troops are drawn from a number of willing countries — they wear blue helmets<br>- peacekeeping role — not allowed to engage in military activity other than to protect themselves<br>- catastrophic failure to act in Srebrenica (Bosnia) |
| Emergency relief | - UNHCR organises refugee camps in conflict zones, e.g. in Jordan due to the Syria conflict (Zaatari camp)<br>- protect vulnerable people from further abuse |

NATO:
- see Table 26 (page 77)

The EU (also see Table 27, page 77) aims to avoid conflict among its member states and to encourage cooperation by:
- enhancing economic interdependence through trade
- providing security where necessary, e.g. through rapid response forces
- policies such as its Foreign Affairs and Security Policy, Common Security and Defence Policy and the European Neighbourhood Policy, by which it aims to cooperate with its close neighbour states in eastern Europe in terms of security, stability and prosperity

NGOs may assist in reducing conflict by:
- monitoring situations and providing early warning of possible conflicts
- direct mediation between parties
- assisting in the strengthening of local institutions, e.g. legal systems
- providing education on accepted norms and behaviours (see Figure 22, page 74)

Treaties:
- see Table 29

> ### Exam tip
> Research the work of one NGO in conflict situations, e.g. the Red Cross, Oxfam.

> ### Key term
> Treaty A written international agreement between two or more states and international organisations.

Table 29 Examples of international treaties regarding global environmental issues

| Environmental issue | Treaty/ies |
|---|---|
| Atmosphere | ■ Montreal Protocol on Substances that Deplete the Ozone Layer: Banned the use of CFCs<br>■ climate change conferences: Kyoto Protocol and the COP21 Agreement |
| Biosphere | Convention on International Trade in Endangered Species of Wild Fauna and Flora (CITES): some successes (Arabian oryx); some failures — illegal trade in ivory and rhino horn has gone 'underground' |
| Oceans | UN Convention on the Law of the Sea (UNCLOS): seeks to manage navigational rights (shipping routes), offshore waters, sea bed resources and ocean areas; it also manages the rights of 42 land-locked states |
| Rivers | UN Convention on the Protection and Use of Trans-boundary Watercourses and International Lakes (the Water Convention): seeks to protect and ensure by cooperation the quantity, quality and sustainable use of trans-boundary water |
| Antarctica | ■ the Antarctic Treaty System (ATS): banned all forms of military activity, and made it a zone free of nuclear tests and disposal of radioactive waste; promoted international scientific research; set aside disputes over land on the continent<br>■ the Protocol on Environmental Protection (Madrid Protocol): an extension of the ATS; banned mining activities (except for scientific research)<br>■ the International Whaling Commission (IWC) and Moratorium (IWM): manage whaling and whale stocks |

> **Key term**
>
> CFCs Chlorofluorocarbons — produced by fridges and aerosols.

# Flows of people, money, ideas and technology

Flows of people and money also move into areas of conflict, and with them come ideas and technology. Examples include:

■ the movement of personnel into conflict zones on peacekeeping missions
■ the transfer of money, e.g. aid donated by member states and/or their people
■ the exchange of ideas regarding strategies and flows of intelligence between organisations involved as they attempt to coordinate effective governance
■ the increasing use of technology, e.g. satellite imagery, remotely controlled drones, weaponry and communications including mobile social networking

## Case study: Global governance strategies

You are required to have **one** case study of an area of conflict to illustrate **strategies for global governance**:

- interventions and interactions of organisations at a range of scales
- the consequences for local communities of global governance of the conflict

a **Interventions and interactions** of different organisations should include:
  - the work of the UN in the area, the national government, and an NGO
  - this involves their specific roles and strategies
  - how they interact in dealing with different aspects of the conflict and its consequences, such as peace and security, and issues such as health, food and water, refugees, human trafficking and exploitation

b **Consequences of global governance** for local communities could include:
  - benefits in the short-term, e.g. provision of shelter, food and fresh water, medicines and hygiene, and personal safety
  - benefits in the longer-term, e.g. training in farming practices
  - unintended effects of military intervention, e.g. increased civilian casualties, population displacement, loss of homes and services, damage to infrastructure, increased violence and escalation of human rights issues

### Exam tip

Note that the intervention strategies used in a conflict situation are often a combination of 'hard' military actions and 'soft' mediation and relief work.

### Exam tip

Examples could include Sudan/South Sudan, Syria and Afghanistan.

# Consequences

## Sovereignty

Table 30 shows the consequences of intervention with respect to sovereignty.

**Table 30 Consequences of intervention with respect to sovereignty**

| Timescale | Consequences |
|---|---|
| Short-term | <ul><li>provision of humanitarian aid, including funds raised through charities</li><li>supply of food, clean water and medical assistance</li><li>providing shelter and assistance for vulnerable refugees, and maintaining peace, law and order</li></ul> |
| Long-term | <ul><li>aimed at resilience-building of all aspects of economic, social and political life</li><li>sustainable development strategies, e.g. agricultural training schemes, education programmes</li><li>post-conflict rehabilitation schemes for affected communities</li><li>changes to political regimes, including the introduction of democracy and elections</li><li>upholding human rights policies, e.g. gender equality issues such as girls in education</li></ul> |

### Key term

**Resilience-building** The means by which a state undergoes transition from a position of fragility to one of greater capability, in which institutional strength and social cohesion enable the promotion of security and development and an ability to respond effectively to shocks.

# Territorial integrity

Table 31 shows the consequences of intervention with respect to territorial integrity.

Table 31 Consequences of intervention with respect to territorial integrity

| Timescale | Consequences |
|---|---|
| Short-term | ■ negotiating periods of ceasefire and maintaining peace<br>■ protecting civilians and providing shelter during conflict<br>■ monitoring the treatment of vulnerable people, e.g. minority groups, women and children (child soldiers) |
| Long-term | ■ aimed at achieving political stability, economic growth and sustainable development<br>■ developing trade and political relationships with other countries<br>■ improving the business environment, e.g. countering corruption and financial mismanagement<br>■ supporting the movement to democracy and fair elections<br>■ adopting international law |

## Exam tips

■ It is difficult to separate sovereignty from territorial integrity — they are interconnected. Questions will often combine them.
■ The specification concentrates on the **intended** effects of intervention, but you should also consider **unintended** effects when discussing this topic.

## Case study: Global governance impact

You are required to have **one** case study of the **impact of global governance of sovereignty or territorial integrity** in one LIDC to illustrate and explain:
■ the sovereignty or territorial integrity issues
■ the global governance strategies used
■ opportunities for stability, growth and development
■ challenges of inequality and injustices

a **Sovereignty or territorial integrity** issues could include:
■ partition of ethnic groups by arbitrary colonial boundaries
■ claims for independence by politically dominant ethnic groups
■ internal conflict including insurgency or coups d'états, terrorism and ineffective state government, which may have marginalised some groups
■ social and economic inequalities in the country that may have contributed

b **Global governance** strategies could include:
■ UN involvement, e.g. peacekeeping missions
■ strengthening government institutions
■ building a stronger human rights culture
■ coordinating the work of regional organisations, NGOs and local government

c **Opportunities** could include:
- improving stability
- strengthening all elements of state legal systems
- protecting human rights
- improving economic growth, perhaps reducing import dependency and gaining access to global supply chains and development
- improving water and food supply and health and education services

d **Challenges** could include:
- inequality, e.g. cultural, socio-economic and urban–rural divisions
- injustice, e.g. human trafficking, drug smuggling, corruption, gender inequality and poverty

## Exam tip

Examples could include African countries, e.g. Mali, Niger, Burkina Faso and Zimbabwe; also Syria and Iraq.

## Do you know?

1 Explain why the River Nile is a potential conflict zone.
2 Through which agencies does the UN provide humanitarian assistance around the world?
3 Summarise the main features of Article 1 of the UN Charter.
4 Outline the role of NGOs in global governance.
5 Identify some long-term benefits of intervention in sovereignty and territorial integrity.

## End of option D questions

1 Outline some unintended effects of military intervention in an area.
2 Outline the economic, environmental and human costs of one post-colonial conflict.
3 National character is an important part of nationalism. Outline the characteristics of one element of national character you have studied.
4 Evaluate this statement: 'In a globalising world, national sovereignty becomes less important.'
5 'For local communities in areas of conflict, intervention can create more problems than it solves.' Discuss.

# Geographical debates: disease dilemmas

## 5.1 Global patterns

**Synoptic links**

Note that in the following two topics synoptic links to other areas of study can be assessed in the AS/A Level examinations. Hence the following two sections feature a number of possible synoptic connections between topics.

### You need to know

- diseases can be classified and their patterns mapped
- the relationship between physical factors and the prevalence of disease can change over time
- natural hazards can influence the outbreak and spread of disease

## Classification and mapping

### Classification

Table 32 shows the terminology used for the spread of diseases.

Table 32 **Disease terminology**

| Disease type | Commentary | Examples |
|---|---|---|
| Infectious/ communicable | ■ spread from person to person, or from a host to a person, directly or indirectly (by a vector)<br>■ caused by bacteria, viruses and parasites | Influenza and the common cold, polio, pneumonia, malaria, tuberculosis (TB), HIV/ AIDS, measles, Zika, Ebola, bilharzia |
| Non-infectious/ non- communicable (NCD) | ■ not spread from one person to another<br>■ linked to diet, lifestyle, age, inherited characteristics and exposure to pollution | Diabetes (all types), all cancers, heart disease and stroke (CVD), cystic fibrosis, asthma, dementia |
| Contagious | ■ an infectious disease — usually associated with human-to-human transmission<br>■ associated with epidemics, pandemics and endemic diseases | The infectious diseases above, also rubella, typhoid, cholera |
| Non-contagious | ■ caused by genetic deficiencies and poor diet, lifestyle and environment | The NCDs above, also sickle cell, leukaemia |

### Key terms

**Vector** An organism that transmits disease from one person/host to another, e.g. a mosquito, tick.

**Epidemic** An outbreak of a disease that can spread quickly in a community or region.

**Pandemic** An epidemic that spreads globally.

**Endemic** A disease that exists permanently in a community or region.

# Global distributions

Malaria:

- in 2015 an estimated 200 million cases of malaria occurred globally and the disease led to over 600,000 deaths (according to WHO)
- an estimated 3.2 billion people (40% of the world's population), in 100 countries, are at risk of being infected with malaria
- of these, 1.2 billion are at high risk (greater than 1-in-1000 chance of getting malaria in a year)
- the burden is heaviest in the WHO African Region, where an estimated 90% of all malaria deaths occur, e.g. DRC (formerly Zaire), Gabon
- children aged under 5 years account for almost 80% of all deaths
- occurs in mainly tropical and sub-tropical regions — areas of rainforest and savanna grasslands with at least 1000 mm of rain per year, and often where the rainfall is seasonal (see page 89)

HIV/AIDS:

- in 2015 an estimated 1.1 million people died from HIV-related causes (WHO)
- over 35 million people live with the disease
- the majority of cases are in sub-Saharan Africa (e.g. Zambia and Botswana)
- other areas of relatively high incidence are southeast Asia, North America and western Europe
- the main determinant of the disease is poverty — areas with limited funding for drugs, medical staff and adult/child education

Tuberculosis:

- in 2015 an estimated 1.8 million people died from TB (WHO)
- the great majority of these deaths were in sub-Saharan Africa
- other areas of high incidence include India, China and Pakistan
- the main determinant is poverty — poor living conditions with overcrowding and poorly ventilated housing, combined with poor medical facilities
- TB deaths are higher when combined with another condition, e.g. HIV/AIDS or diabetes (0.4 million deaths from TB/HIV in 2015)

Type 2 diabetes:

- the total number of people in the world with T2D is projected to rise from over 400 million in 2015 to almost 600 million in 2035
- it is estimated that 80% of the people who have T2D live in EDCs, e.g. India and China
- T2D is linked to 8% of total world mortality — the same as HIV/AIDS and malaria combined

## Exam tip

Examination questions are likely to use world maps in relation to these diseases — make sure you know your continents and countries.

## Key terms

**WHO** World Health Organization.

**HIV** Human immunodeficiency virus.

**AIDS** Acquired immune deficiency syndrome.

- mortality and disability associated with T2D are particularly high in EDCs and LIDCs, where people are unlikely to get the treatments that help prevent the worst complications of the disease
- the main determinant is lifestyle — diets with a high fat and salt content, and lack of physical exercise, cause obesity; being overweight can lead to T2D

**Exam tip**

Type 1 diabetes is not as prevalent, or increasing as rapidly, as T2D.

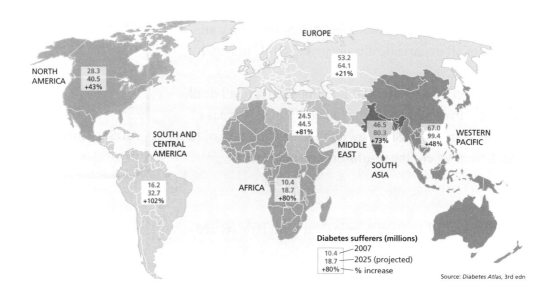

**Figure 25** Global distribution of people aged 20–79 with diabetes (all types; millions) 2007 and 2025 (projected)

Cardiovascular disease:

- in 2015 over 17 million people died from CVD (WHO)
- deaths are more common in older age groups, though premature deaths are higher in EDCs and LIDCs
- premature deaths are high in the Middle East, south Asia, eastern Europe and sub-Saharan Africa
- the main determinants are age and lifestyle — alcohol and tobacco abuse, poor diet and a lack of physical exercise
- lack of healthcare and education are also contributory factors

## Disease diffusion

Although originally based on the spread of agricultural innovation in Sweden, the Hägerstrand model has been applied to disease diffusion:

- primary stage: certain areas have a disease but the rest of the population/area has no sign

**Synoptic link**

Consider the degree to which the distribution of diseases may be linked to global economic systems.

**Exam tip**

Up-to-date information on all of the above diseases can be obtained from www.who.int/topics/en

**Key term**

Diffusion The process by which a disease spreads from its source.

- diffusion stage: the disease spreads to new populations/areas
- condensing stage: the number of new cases becomes equal in all parts of a population/area
- saturation stage: the disease reaches its peak and diffusion decreases

Diffusion phases:
- expansion diffusion: the disease spreads from one area to another, remaining and intensifying in the source area
- relocation diffusion: the disease moves to another area, leaving the source area
- contagious diffusion: diffusion occurs from direct contact with a carrier and is greater in an area close to the original source
- hierarchical diffusion: diffusion spreads down an established order, e.g. from a large city to small villages

Diffusion barriers can be:
- physical, e.g. mountain ranges, seas/oceans, extensive deserts, climatic conditions
- socio-economic, e.g. governmental strategies to address an outbreak/epidemic, controls at borders (quarantine), vaccination programmes, health education

# Physical factors

Several writers have sought to examine links between the natural environment and the incidence of disease.

## Climate, relief and climate change

Some points regarding climate and relief with regard to malaria and influenza:
- malaria is a disease associated with a tropical climate
- the malaria parasite (*Plasmodium falciparum*) needs temperatures of 16°–32°C to develop
- the key is the existence of a particular form of mosquito (female *Anopheles*) that spreads the malaria parasite — the vector
- these mosquitoes breed in warm areas of stagnant water, and hence are common in flat lowland marshy areas
- some regions have a fairly constant number of cases of malaria throughout the year (malaria endemic)
- other areas have 'malaria seasons', usually coinciding with the rainy season (monsoon) and high humidity
- in Roman times mosquitoes and cases of malaria were relatively common in lowland marshy areas of southern France, coastal

> **Synoptic link**
>
> Consider inter-linkages between incidence of disease and the physical landscape you have studied.

Spain, mainland Italy and Sicily; subsequent drainage of these areas has markedly reduced the prevalence of the disease
- the incidence of malaria decreases at altitudes over 1500 m — hence some tropical areas are unaffected, e.g. the Kenyan Highlands
- the influenza virus (prevalent in temperate climates) is more efficient in colder temperatures and at times of low relative humidity

Climate change:
- **emergent** and changing distributions of vector-borne diseases are issues associated with climate change
- it is predicted that the prevalence of some existing diseases, e.g. malaria and dengue fever, will increase as mosquito vectors spread further around the world following warmer and wetter weather
- areas most at risk include Turkey, China, Mexico and the southern USA
- in addition, it is thought that other emergent diseases could have a greater incidence, e.g. the Zika virus in Latin America, West Nile virus in North America and Lyme disease (spread by ticks) within Europe (including the UK)

## Water sources

Key points:
- preventing the spread of water quality-related disease is a major global health challenge — almost 1 billion people lack access to a safe, clean water supply
- two million deaths annually are attributable to unsafe water, sanitation and hygiene, and almost half of these are from diarrhoeal diseases
- more than 50 countries a year report cholera to WHO
- **schistosomiasis** has infected an estimated 260 million people

## Zoonotic

Key points:
- **zoonotic diseases** are caused by bacteria (e.g. salmonella, E.coli), viruses (e.g. rabies, avian flu) and parasites
- they are transmitted by direct contact (e.g. bites), insect vectors (e.g. mosquitoes) and contaminated food or water (e.g. faecal contamination)

---

### Exam tip

Note that many other tropical diseases also flourish in hot, wet, humid weather: dengue fever, West Nile virus, sleeping sickness, Zika and Ebola. Once again it is because the vector, a mosquito or tsetse fly, can breed easily in these regions.

### Synoptic link

Consider connections between changes in the water and carbon cycles and the diseases you have studied.

### Key terms

**Emergent disease** A disease that has existed previously with a low incidence, which is now increasing rapidly.

**Schistosomiasis (bilharzia)** A disease associated with parasitic worms that live in irrigation ditches and water courses.

**Zoonotic disease** Disease directly transmitted from animals to humans, e.g. rabies, bird flu.

## Case study: Natural hazards and disease

You are required to have **one** case study of a country that has experienced a **natural hazard** (e.g. an earthquake, drought or monsoon rains) to illustrate how a natural hazard can influence the outbreak and spread of a named disease, e.g. cholera or typhoid.

Your case study must illustrate:

■ the geographical area affected by the hazard and its influence on the risk and outbreak of the chosen disease
■ environmental factors affecting the spread of the disease, e.g. climate, sanitation levels, water supply and food
■ human factors affecting the spread of the disease, e.g. population density, access to clean water and immunisation programmes
■ the impacts of the disease on resident populations
■ strategies used to minimise impacts of the disease at both national and international scales

### Synoptic link

Consider the influence of 'character of place' when studying an outbreak of a disease.

### Exam tip

Possible examples include Haiti (a cholera outbreak following the 2010 earthquake), Bangladesh (various flooding events linked to epidemics of water-borne diseases such as diarrhoea and typhoid).

### Do you know?

1 How is malaria transmitted?
2 What is Type 1 diabetes?
3 To what extent is the disease Ebola a function of climate?
4 Outline the possible impact of the El NiÒo effect on diseases.
5 Describe the incidence of one zoonotic disease.

# 5.2 Links to development

### You need to know

■ as countries develop the frequency of communicable diseases decreases
■ as countries develop the frequency of non-communicable diseases (NCDs) increases

## The epidemiological transition

Key points:

■ this model relating to population, health and disease was put forward by Omran in 1971

- the model states that societies undergo three 'ages' of health:
  - □ an age of pestilence and famine: a period in which mortality is high, with the principle causes of death being infectious diseases and poor maternal conditions reinforced by nutritional deficiencies
  - □ an age of receding pandemics: socio-economic developments and advances in medical science and healthcare (e.g. better public water supplies and penicillin) mean infectious diseases are reduced and life expectancy increases
  - □ an age of degenerative diseases: as infectious diseases are controlled and people live longer, there is an increased incidence of degenerative diseases (cancers, heart disease); diseases associated with modernisation and industrialisation (obesity, diabetes) also begin to increase
- a fourth stage has been added — an age of delayed degenerative diseases, in which the causes of death are generally the same as in the third stage (although dementia is more prevalent) but they occur later in the life cycle as life expectancy increases
- Omran stated that socio-economic development is responsible for the movement of a society through these 'ages', from high fertility and mortality rates (with young populations and high levels of infectious disease) to societies with low fertility and mortality rates (with ageing populations where NCDs predominate)

## Advanced countries and low-income developing countries

Table 33 provides a comparison of deaths and morbidity in ACs and LIDCs.

Table 33 Comparing deaths and morbidity in ACs and LIDCs

| ACs | LIDCs |
| --- | --- |
| ACs have higher proportions of deaths and morbidity from NCDs, due to: <br><br> - successful reduction and/or elimination of communicable diseases — due to advances in clean water provision and medical treatments <br> - high standards of living, including good sanitation and nutrition <br> - education and awareness of potential harmful conditions <br> - behavioural risk factors, such as tobacco and alcohol abuse <br> - sedentary lifestyles <br> - increasing longevity, which creates a higher proportion of degenerative diseases | LIDCs have higher proportions of deaths and morbidity from communicable diseases, due to: <br><br> - lack of funds for state governments to intervene in health matters <br> - inadequate sanitation and limited access to clean water <br> - reduced access to education or good diets — malnutrition and under-nutrition are common <br> - higher incidences of transmittable disease caused by vectors, e.g. mosquitoes <br> - poor housing and overcrowding |

### Key terms

**Morbidity** Illness that includes any diseased state, disability or condition of poor health.

**Malnutrition** A diet with a deficiency of nutrients, e.g. vitamin D (causes rickets), vitamin B (beriberi) and vitamin C (scurvy).

### Exam tip

It is important to note that NCDs are also increasing in incidence in LIDCs — the main difference being that they occur earlier in the life cycle for many people.

## Case study: Air pollution

You are required to have **one** case study of a country that is experiencing **air pollution and the impact of air pollution** on incidence of cancers (e.g. lung or bladder cancer).

For your chosen country you should illustrate:
- the causes of air pollution
- the impact of air pollution on incidence of cancers
- possible national and global solutions

### Exam tip

Possible examples include China, India or the UK.

### Synoptic link

There is a clear connection here between global economic systems and mortality/morbidity.

### Do you know?

1 Give an alternative name for non-communicable diseases such as obesity, lung cancer and CVD. (Clue — development.)
2 Distinguish between 'under-nutrition' and 'over-nutrition'.

# 5.3 Management

### You need to know

- communicable diseases have causes and impacts with mitigation and response strategies
- non-communicable diseases have causes and impacts with mitigation and response strategies
- increasing mobility impacts on diffusion of disease and the ability to respond to it
- physical barriers may affect mitigation strategies to combat global pandemics

## Case study: Communicable diseases

You are required to have **one** case study of a **communicable disease** (e.g. malaria or TB) at a country scale, either an LIDC or an EDC.

Your case study should illustrate:
- the environmental and human causes of the disease
- the prevalence, incidence and patterns of the disease
- the socio-economic impacts of the disease
- government and international agencies' direct and indirect strategies to mitigate against the disease
- the varying levels of success of these strategies

## Example: malaria

General points:

- for the environmental causes and prevalence of malaria, see page 89
- Table 34 shows socio-economic variables influencing a high incidence of malaria

Table 34 Socio-economic variables influencing a high incidence of malaria

| Variable | Commentary |
|---|---|
| Housing quality | Densely clustered and overcrowded dwellings increase incidence |
| Unsanitary conditions | Areas with standing dirty water, open waste flows and outlets encourage more mosquitoes |
| Occupation | Some jobs are more prone to infection, such as farm workers and irrigation workers |
| Level of education | Researchers have found that in general people who have not completed their primary education are more likely to catch malaria |

Socio-economic impacts:

- health:
    - the common first symptoms — fever, headache, chills and vomiting — appear 10 to 15 days after a person is infected
    - if not treated promptly with effective medicines, malaria can cause severe illness that is often fatal
    - the disease also contributes to childhood anaemia, a major cause of limited growth and development
- other impacts:
    - further high personal impacts, such as the spending on ITNs, doctors' fees, drugs and transport to health facilities
    - disrupted schooling and employment through absenteeism
    - nutrition deficiencies and anaemia in women in malarial regions — in some areas 25% of first babies have a low birth weight
    - the disease may account for as much as 40% of public health expenditure, 30–50% of inpatient admissions and up to 60% of outpatient visits

Mitigation strategies:

- malaria control, and ultimately its elimination, are inextricably linked with strengthening of health systems, infrastructure development and poverty reduction
- interventions include:
    - vector controls (which reduce transmission by the mosquito from humans to mosquitoes and then back to humans) achieved using ITNs, LLINs or IRS

### Exam tip

Possible examples include malaria in any sub-Saharan country, or cholera in Haiti. You could use the same case study you studied in Section 5.1 Global patterns (page 91).

### Synoptic link

Consider the influence of 'character of place' when studying the cause(s), impacts and management of a communicable disease.

### Key terms

ITN Insecticide-treated mosquito net.

LLIN Long-lasting insecticidal nets.

IRS Indoor residual spraying.

- ☐ chemoprevention (which prevents the blood infections in humans)
- ☐ expansion in the use of diagnostic testing and the deployment of ACTs — this indicates a move away from treating people who *have* the disease to those who *might* have it
- ☐ ensuring pregnant women receive preventative treatment during their pregnancy in order to reduce child deaths

How successful has this been?
- see page 87 for the current state of global mortality from malaria
- in 2015 a record number of LLINs were delivered to endemic countries in Africa
- emerging drug- and insecticide-resistance poses a major threat and, if left unaddressed, could trigger an upsurge in the disease
- resistance to artemisinin has been detected in southeast Asian countries, e.g. Cambodia, Thailand and Vietnam
- in 2015 US scientists stated that they had bred a genetically modified mosquito that could resist malaria infection — if the laboratory technique works in the field, it could offer a new way of stopping the mosquitoes from spreading malaria

**Key term**

ACT Artemisinin-based combination therapies.

## Case study: Non-communicable diseases

You are required to have **one** case study of a **non-communicable disease** (e.g. CVD or T2D) at a country scale, either an AC or an EDC.

Your case study should illustrate:
- the social, economic and cultural causes of the disease
- the prevalence, incidence and patterns of the disease
- the socio-economic impacts of the disease
- government and international agencies' direct and indirect strategies to mitigate against the disease
- the varying levels of success of these strategies

## Example: type 2 diabetes

General points relating to T2D in EDCs (see also page 87):
- WHO states that overweight and obesity are driving the global T2D epidemic
- recent estimates suggest that 1 billion people in EDCs are obese
- Table 35 shows socio-economic variables influencing a high incidence of T2D

Table 35 Socio-economic variables influencing a high incidence of T2D

| Variable | Commentary |
|---|---|
| Diet | High calorie intake is the main factor leading to obesity — rapid economic development has introduced a more 'Western' diet to EDCs, with fewer fruit and vegetables and a higher intake of carbohydrates, fatty foods, salt and sugar |
| Urban lifestyle | Rates of urbanisation in EDCs are considerably higher than elsewhere — this tends to lead to a more sedentary lifestyle, with a low level of physical activity |
| Tobacco use | Smoking is a key risk factor linked to T2D: an estimated 50–60% of adult males in EDCs are regular smokers |
| Stress | Stress increases blood glucose levels, raises blood pressure and can suppress the digestive process — raised blood sugar levels are a key risk factor in the development of T2D |

Socio-economic impacts:
- health:
  - T2D cannot be cured but it can be managed with a mixture of medication and lifestyle change
  - in the longer term it can lead to heart disease, kidney failure, blindness and, in extreme cases, lower-limb amputation
- other impacts:
  - as most healthcare costs in EDCs must be paid by patients out-of-pocket, the cost of healthcare for T2D creates significant strain on household budgets, particularly for lower-income families
  - treatment for diabetes can be protracted and therefore extremely expensive for individuals and their families

Mitigation strategies and success:
- public awareness of T2D is slowly increasing in many EDCs
- for example, in Sri Lanka awareness is increasing mainly because of local media coverage and the activities of the Diabetes Association of Sri Lanka (DASL)
- DASL has a walk-in centre in the capital Colombo, where individuals can be screened or take part in structured health programmes at a modest cost; it provides information through workshops, a website and printed materials
- DASL is also spreading the message that exercise can help reduce the threat of T2D

**Exam tip**

Possible examples include any form of cancer in the UK, or T2D in Sri Lanka or India.

**Synoptic link**

Consider the influence of 'character of place' when studying the cause(s), impacts and management of an NCD.

# Responding to disease
## International organisations

A number of international organisations seek to take action to combat disease, including predicting diseases, gathering data, research and support programmes. They include:

- WHO
- UNICEF
- Joint United Nations Programme on HIV/AIDS (UNAIDS)

A number of internationally sponsored NGOs are also involved, including:

- Médecins Sans Frontières (MSF)
- Oxfam
- charity organisations sponsored by wealthy individuals, e.g. the Bill and Melinda Gates Foundation

The WHO:

- is an agency of the UN, established in 1948 and based in Geneva, to further international cooperation for improved health conditions
- provides a central clearing house for information and research, for example on vaccines, cancer research, nutrition, drug addiction and nuclear radiation hazards
- sponsors measures for the control of epidemics and endemic diseases by promoting mass campaigns involving vaccination programmes, instruction on the use of antibiotics, assistance in providing pure water supplies and sanitation systems and health education for rural populations
- advises on the prevention and treatment of both infectious diseases and NCDs
- works with other UN agencies (e.g. UNAIDS and UNICEF) and NGOs on international health issues and crises (e.g. the Ebola crisis in 2014/15)

> ### Key terms
>
> **UNICEF** United Nations International Children's Emergency Fund.
>
> **SARS** Severe acute respiratory syndrome.

> ### Exam tip
>
> You should be prepared to evaluate the contribution and roles of international organisations in the mitigation of disease.

## An international disease outbreak

For example, the **SARS** outbreak of 2002/03. Key points:

- SARS is an infectious disease spread through respiratory functions, e.g. sneezing and coughing
- the 2002/03 outbreak involved more than 30 countries and over 700 deaths
- it originated in southern China and initially spread into Hong Kong, Vietnam, and Singapore
- further cases appeared in Canada, the USA and Australia — spread by air travel
- in July 2003, WHO declared the disease 'contained'

## Case study: Responding to disease

You are required to have **one** case study of the **role of one NGO in dealing with a disease outbreak** within a country, including the local level.

For your chosen example, illustrate:
- the causes and effects of the outbreak
- the NGO's response — including its overall strategy for the country and its specific work with local communities and households
- a number of NGOs operate in the field of world health
- in some EDCs and LIDCs they often act as alternative healthcare providers to the state — during crises they provide the initial response, particularly in remote areas
- they are largely funded by donations from ACs, mostly from individuals or organisations rather than from nations

### Example: Médecins Sans Frontières

MSF:
- is a worldwide movement, with 90% of its income coming from individual donations, which allows it to stay independent and impartial
- works in over 60 countries, with specialist teams ready for any health emergency
- monitors epidemics on the ground continuously and is able to mount rapid emergency responses
- in 2014, for example, treated over 47,000 people in 16 cholera outbreaks — it provided beds, plastic sheeting, oral rehydration salts and surgical equipment
- managed a meningitis outbreak in Niger where 350 patients were treated on a daily basis

### Exam tip

Possible examples include the Red Cross (Haiti) and MSF (Niger).

# Dealing with global pandemics
## Physical barriers

Key points:
- physical barriers affecting disease mitigation strategies include mountain ranges, seas and oceans, deserts and extreme climates
- remoteness of communities can have positive and negative effects on mitigation strategies (Table 36)

**Table 36** Positive and negative effects of physical barriers on mitigation strategies

| Positive | Negative |
|---|---|
| ▪ population movement across these barriers is limited<br>▪ most vectors do not travel across them<br>▪ infection rates are often low<br>▪ easier to contain an outbreak | ▪ difficult to move medical assistance into an affected area — humanitarian aid is delayed<br>▪ when flooding occurs, e.g. due to monsoonal rains, breeding conditions for vectors improve<br>▪ flooding also restricts access by aid workers<br>▪ isolation reduces immunity, and so when a disease does arrive, resistance is low and incidence is high |

# Government strategies

See mitigation strategies for malaria (page 94).

At an international level, WHO provides:

- assessment of risk, response and recovery actions based on surveillance and monitoring of previous outbreaks
- encouragement and advice on creating a national pandemic-preparedness plan
- advice on selection of strains for new vaccine production
- guidance on treatment of patients, establishing education programmes and use of rapid diagnostic tests for screening at a country's entry or exit points
- plans for high-density populations, e.g. refugee camps, including public health advice regarding social distancing, hand hygiene and household ventilation

At a national level, the UK government provides:

- public guidance for international travel
- guidance for businesses and workplaces
- coordination of essential services, businesses, media, other public, private and voluntary organisations and local communities
- encouragement of the public to follow government advice by adopting basic hygiene measures and reducing personal risk of catching or spreading a virus
- prediction of impacts, such as the probable number of infected people, number of additional deaths, and social and economic disruption

## Do you know?

1 What is the difference between a communicable and a non-communicable disease?

2 Outline the work of UNICEF.

3 How can an earthquake hinder disease mitigation?

# 5.4 Can diseases be eradicated?

## You need to know

■ nature has provided medicines to treat disease over a long period of time

■ 'top down' and 'bottom up' strategies deal with disease risk and eradication

## Natural medicines

Table 37 shows examples of medical drugs and their natural origins.

Table 37 Examples of medical drugs and their natural origins

| Drug | Source | Soil type | Climate | Uses |
|------|--------|-----------|---------|------|
| Morphine | Opium poppy | Clays and well-drained soils rich in humus | Warm humid weather, temperatures over 30°C | Pain relief |
| Quinine | Cinchona tree | Fertile soils with organic matter (rainforest soils) | Temperatures over 20°C, wet humid conditions (over 2000 mm a year) | Treating malaria |
| Ginseng | Ginseng plant | As above — rainforest soils | As above — tropical climate | Energiser, stimulant, aphrodisiac |
| Digitalis | Foxglove | Fertile, humus-rich soils | Temperate climate | Heart problems — stimulates blood flow |

## Case study: Medicinal plants

You are required to have **one** case study of one **medicinal plant**.

For your chosen example, you should be able to illustrate its:

■ growing conditions
■ medicinal importance for the treatment of disease
■ international trade (legal and/or illegal)
■ sustainability of use

### Exam tip

Possible examples include rosy periwinkle, cinchona tree, opium poppy, yew bark, magnolia and foxglove.

## Conservation issues

Growing demand for plants for natural medicines and cures is causing concern regarding the sustainability of their use, and creating conservation issues:

■ over-harvesting of wild plants
■ the need to obtain (or cultivate) samples for continued R&D of new products

■ habitat loss resulting from deforestation of tropical rainforest
■ diminishing genetic and biodiversity
■ species survival and/or extinction
■ disruption to or destruction of natural ecosystems

## Case study: Pharmaceutical transnationals

You are required to have **one** case study of the **global impact of a pharmaceutical TNC**.

For your chosen TNC you should be able to illustrate its:
■ research and development (R&D) strategies, including any scientific breakthroughs
■ patented drugs
■ drug manufacture
■ global flows of distribution

# Global and national strategies

Key points:
■ the **eradication** of several diseases is an overall aim of WHO (a **top-down** approach)
■ it has been achieved only for a minority of diseases, e.g. smallpox
■ other diseases are tracked to see whether they can be eradicated by:
  □ identifying their host/transmission route
  □ possible intervention strategies
  □ discovering the timing and spatial extent of distribution
■ eradication depends on finance and national political will, however

# Grassroots strategies

Grassroot strategies (**bottom-up**) are often considered to be more effective interventions:

■ they are self-motivated among local communities, where need is often greatest
■ they are a more sustainable approach — local people have a vested interest in accepting responsibility for their own health
■ they are achieved through education and training
■ in many LIDCs and EDCs, where gender inequalities restrict development, the empowerment of women has led to their increased involvement in community health

## Do you know?

1 What has been done to conserve flora and fauna for medical research?
2 How does WHO seek to eradicate a disease?
3 Outline the eradication of one disease at a national scale that you have studied.
4 Distinguish between 'eradication' and 'elimination'.

## End of section 5 questions

1 Explain the concept of disease diffusion.
2 Describe the global distribution of one NCD you have studied.
3 Explain how global patterns of temperature and precipitation affect patterns of disease.
4 Explain why malnutrition is widespread in certain parts of the world.
5 Discuss the impacts of one non-communicable disease on health, economic development and lifestyle.
6 Suggest why one country experiencing air pollution has seen incidences of disease change over time.
7 'Affluence is one of the main causes of non-communicable disease.' To what extent do you agree with this statement?
8 Discuss the role of pharmaceutical transnational corporations with regard to global health matters.
9 Examine how far the same physical factors influence disease outbreaks and landscape systems.
10 'It is more challenging to mitigate against communicable diseases in areas with territorial integrity conflicts.' How far do you agree with the statement?

# 6 Geographical debates: hazardous Earth

## 6.1 Theoretical background

**You need to know**
- there is a variety of evidence for the theories of continental drift and plate tectonics
- there are distinctive features and processes at plate boundaries

## Theory and evidence

### The Earth's structure

The Earth's structure (Figure 26) consists of:
- an outer layer (crust) split up into seven large, rigid plates and several smaller ones, all of which are able to move slowly on the surface
- a middle layer (mantle) — some have suggested that the crust/mantle division is more complicated and split into the lithosphere and the asthenosphere
- the centre (core) — very hot molten rock (over 5,000°C)

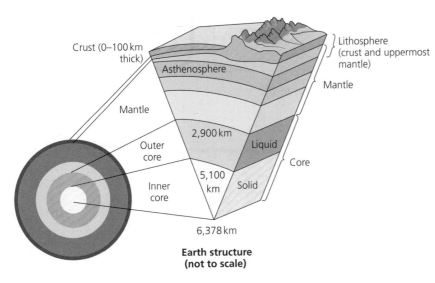

Figure 26 **The structure of the Earth**

# Plate tectonic theory and evidence

Table 38 shows the plate tectonics theories and discoveries.

Table 38 Plate tectonics theories/discoveries

| Theory/discovery | Commentary |
|---|---|
| Wegener's Continental Drift hypothesis (1912) | Postulated that now-separate continents were once joined together |
| Previous glaciations in southern Africa, Australia, South America and India | Suggest that these land masses were once joined together in a more polar location |
| Fossils of the reptile mesosaurus found in both western South Africa and eastern Brazil, and fossils of certain brachiopods found in limestones in both Australia and India | Suggest that each of these two sets of areas were once joined together but have since drifted apart |
| Holmes (1930s) stated that Earth's internal radioactive heat was the driving force of convection currents in the mantle that could move tectonic plates | It is thought that radioactive decay of isotopes uranium-238 and thorium-232 in the Earth's core and mantle generate huge amounts of heat |
| The discovery (1960s) of the asthenosphere | A weak, deformable layer beneath the rigid lithosphere |
| The discovery (1960s) of magnetic stripes in the oceanic crust of the sea bed; the rocks in these stripes become progressively older from the mid-oceanic ridges | Palaeomagnetic (ancient magnetism) signals from past reversals of the Earth's magnetic field prove that new crust is created by the process of sea-floor spreading at mid-ocean ridges |
| Elevated altitudes of oceanic crust at ridges at divergent plate boundaries | Create a 'slope', down which oceanic plates slide (gravitational sliding) |
| High density ocean floor is being dragged down by a downward gravitational force (slab pull) beneath the adjoining continental crust at convergent boundaries | Creates subduction zones |

Note: All of this remains a theory because scientists have not yet directly observed the interior of the Earth.

# Features and processes
## Global distribution

Key features:
- tectonic hazards (volcanoes, earthquakes, tsunamis) occur at specific points that are usually associated with tectonic plate boundaries (margins) (Figure 27)

- their distribution is uneven — some areas of the world are at high risk and others are at low risk
- hazards occur at either divergent plate boundaries, convergent plate boundaries or conservative plate boundaries
- earthquakes also occur where the Indo-Australian plate collides with the Eurasian plate — a collision zone

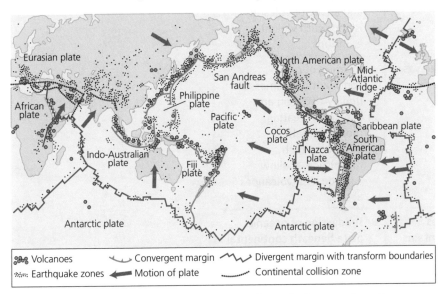

**Figure 27** The global distribution of plate boundaries, earthquakes and volcanoes

## Distinctive plate margins

Table 39 shows distinctive plate boundary settings and associated hazards.

**Table 39** Distinctive plate boundary settings and associated hazards

| Boundary/margin type | Plate type | Example | Description/hazards |
|---|---|---|---|
| Divergent/constructive | Oceanic/oceanic | Mid-Atlantic Ridge (e.g. Ascension Island and Iceland) | <ul><li>rising convection currents bring magma to the surface, forcing two plates apart and creating ocean ridges</li><li>small rift valleys are created along the ridges</li><li>basaltic eruptions; low viscosity of lava (pillow lavas)</li><li>'black smokers' — jets of hot water rich in minerals</li><li>low magnitude, shallow (<70 km) earthquakes</li></ul> |
| | Continent/continent | East African Rift Valley/Red Sea | <ul><li>mantle plume splitting continental plate to create rift valleys (graben)</li><li>basaltic volcanoes and low magnitude earthquakes</li></ul> |

## Exam tip

Make sure you know some examples of plate boundaries, the types of plates (oceanic/continental) involved and the direction of movement of each of them.

## Key terms

**Divergent (constructive) boundaries** Where new crust is generated as the plates pull away from each other.

**Convergent (destructive) boundaries** Where crust is destroyed as one plate dives under another.

**Conservative boundaries** Where crust is neither produced nor destroyed as the plates slide horizontally past each other.

**Rift valley** A linear steep-sided valley formed by the sinking down of rocks between fractures and faults.

**Graben** The down-faulted section of a rift valley.

| Boundary/ margin type | Plate type | Example | Description/hazards |
|---|---|---|---|
| Convergent/ Destructive | Oceanic/ oceanic | Aleutian Islands | ■ subduction of one plate beneath another<br>■ deep sea trench formed<br>■ frequent earthquakes and an arc of volcanic islands with violent eruptions |
| | Continent/ continent (collision) | Himalayas | ■ meeting of two continental landmasses (Indo-Australian and Eurasian), creating mountain belt<br>■ infrequent high magnitude, shallow earthquakes; volcanoes absent |
| | Oceanic/ continent | Andes mountains | ■ subduction of oceanic plate beneath continental plate<br>■ deep sea trenches (6000–11,000 m) and fold mountain ranges<br>■ frequent deep (up to 700 km) high magnitude earthquakes and violent volcanoes due to high viscosity of lava |
| Conservative | Oceanic/ continent | San Andreas Fault | ■ plates slide past each other along transform faults<br>■ frequent shallow, and some high magnitude, earthquakes; volcanoes absent |

## Key term

Transform faults  Cracks and tears at right angles to plate movement.

## Exam tip

One revision strategy is to sketch and annotate diagrams of different plate boundaries.

## Do you know?

1 State two differences between oceanic and continental plates.

2 Explain why some geologists suggest that Iceland is more than just located on a mid-oceanic ridge.

3 Why is plate tectonics still just a theory?

4 Which type of plate boundary produces the most hazardous volcanoes?

5 What is palaeomagnetism and how does it support the idea of sea-floor spreading?

# 6.2 Volcanic hazards

## You need to know
- there is a variety of volcanic activity and resultant landforms and landscapes
- there are distinctive hazards resulting from volcanoes

## Types of volcano

Key features (see also Table 39, page 105, for plate dynamics):
- volcanoes are built by the accumulation of their own eruptive products: lava, bombs (crusted-over ash deposits) and tephra (airborne ash and dust); gases are also emitted
- a volcano is most commonly a conical mountain built around a vent that connects with reservoirs of molten rock below the surface
- a few volcanoes erupt more or less continuously (e.g. Mauna Loa, Hawaii), but others lie dormant between eruptions
- the type of volcano and volcanic activity depends upon the nature of the lava (Table 40):
  - if the lava is a thin fluid (low viscosity), then gases escape easily (effusive eruptions)
  - if the lava is thick and dense (high viscosity), the gases will not escape freely but will build up tremendous pressure (explosive eruptions)

### Key term

**Viscosity** Describes ease of flow: acid lavas are viscous (sticky), basaltic lavas are less viscous (runny).

Table 40 Variations in the type of volcanic activity in relation to types of lava

| | Basaltic lava | Andesitic lava | Rhyolitic lava |
|---|---|---|---|
| Silica content | 45–50% | 55–60% | 65% |
| Eruption temperature | 1,000°C+ | 800°C | 700°C |
| Viscosity and gas content | Very runny, low gas | Sticky, intermediate gas | Very sticky, high gas |
| Volcanic products | Very hot, runny lava Shield volcanoes Low land or plateaux | Sticky lava flows, tephra, ash, gas Composite volcanoes | Pyroclastic flows, gas and volcanic ash Dome volcanoes |
| Eruption interval | Can be almost continuous, e.g. Hawaii | Decades or centuries | Millennia |

| | Basaltic lava | Andesitic lava | Rhyolitic lava |
|---|---|---|---|
| Tectonic setting and plate margins | Oceanic hot spots and constructive margins | Destructive plate margins — oceanic/ continental and oceanic/oceanic | Continental hot spots and continental/ continental margins |
| Processes | Dry partial melting of the upper mantle/lower lithosphere<br><br>Basaltic magma is generally uncontaminated by water, etc. | Wet partial melting of subducting oceanic crust contaminated by water and other material as magma rises | In situ melting of lower continental crust<br><br>Most rhyolitic (granitic) magmas cool before they reach the surface |
| Hazardous? | Not really | Very | Very (but rare) |

# Magma plumes

Some volcanoes do not occur at plate boundaries (e.g. Hawaii and the Galápagos Islands):

■ earthquakes can occur in mid-plate settings, usually associated with ancient fault lines being re-activated by tectonic stresses
■ volcanoes can occur at hot spots — isolated plumes of convecting heat (mantle plumes) rise towards the surface, generating basaltic volcanoes
■ a mantle plume is stationary, but the tectonic plate above moves slowly over it
■ over millennia, this produces a chain of volcanic islands, with extinct ones most distant from the plume location

# Super-volcanoes

Key points:

■ evidence of past impacts of high-magnitude events from super-volcanoes comes from monitoring previous ash spread and depth
■ paleo-biological assessments of effects on ecosystems, e.g. mass mortalities, also provide evidence
■ the most recent event was 27,000 years ago, at Taupo (North Island, New Zealand)
■ some suggest a similar event in Yellowstone (Wyoming, USA) is likely to occur

# Magnitude

■ measured by the volcanic explosivity index (VEI) and based on the volume, duration and column height of ejections

## Key terms

Hot spot An area where heat under the Earth's crust is localised — at such points, rising magma can produce volcanoes.

Super-volcano A volcano that erupts over more than $1000 \, km^3$ in a single eruption event.

## Exam tip

The OCR specification states that volcanoes in the east African Rift Valley are on hot spots — geologists, however, believe they are on a divergent (constructive) plate boundary (Table 39, page 105).

- can be related back to the type of plate boundary the volcano is located on:
  - ☐ effusive eruptions of basaltic lavas with low VEI (0 to 3) are associated with constructive boundaries or plumes
  - ☐ explosive eruptions of andesitic or rhyolitic lava with high VEI (4 to 7) are associated with destructive boundaries

# Hazards

Volcanic hazards include (Figure 28):

- lava flows: not usually a major threat as molten lava; create extensive areas of solidified lava
- pyroclastic flows: very hot (800°C), high-velocity flows (over $200\,km\,h^{-1}$) of a mixture of gases and tephra that devastate everything in their path
- ash falls (tephra): solid material of varying grain size (from fine ash up to volcanic bombs) ejected into the atmosphere; buildings often collapse under weight of ash falling on to their roofs; air, thick with ash, is very difficult to breathe in and can cause respiratory problems
- nuées ardentes: glowing clouds of hot gas, steam, dust, volcanic ash and larger pyroclasts produced during a violent eruption; can travel at high velocity
- volcanic gases: include carbon dioxide, carbon monoxide, hydrogen sulphide, sulphur dioxide and chlorine; can be poisonous and contribute to acid rain

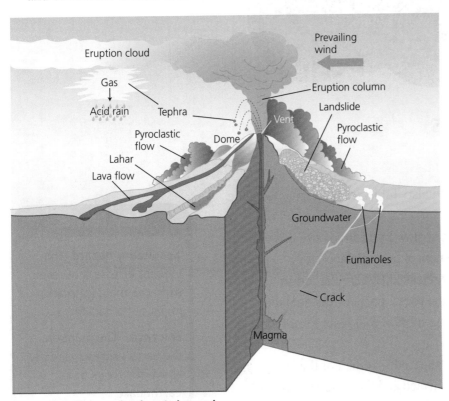

**Figure 28** Types of volcanic hazard

Volcanoes also produce secondary hazards:

- mud flows (lahars): occur when rain mobilises deposits of volcanic ash
- flooding: caused by the melting of ice caps and glaciers, such as glacial bursts (jökulhlaup in Iceland)
- tsunamis: violent eruptions in coastal areas can displace the water nearby — very rare
- climate cooling: some eruptions (e.g. Mount Pinatubo, 1991) eject huge quantities of ash into the upper atmosphere, which can block the energy of the sun

> **Exam tip**
>
> A volcano's impact can be judged in terms of its primary and secondary effects, and the environmental, social, economic and political consequences, short and long term. Make sure you include these in your case studies of volcanic events (see page 113).

> **Do you know?**
>
> 1 Describe the global distribution of volcanoes.
> 2 Why did the Eyjafjallaj^kull eruption have such a great impact on the world?
> 3 Why is lava chemistry important in influencing the potential danger of a volcano?

# 6.3 Seismic hazards

> **You need to know**
>
> - there is a variety of earthquake activity and resultant landforms and landscapes
> - there are distinctive hazards resulting from earthquakes

## Characteristics

### Causes

Key features (Figure 29, and see also Table 39, page 105, for plate dynamics):

- as the Earth's crust is mobile, a slow build-up of stress within the rocks can exist where movement is taking place
- when this stress is suddenly released (where the strain overcomes the elasticity of the rock), parts of the surface experience an intense shaking motion that lasts for a few seconds — an earthquake
- large amounts of energy are released — much of the energy is transferred vertically to the surface and then moves outwards from the epicentre as seismic waves

> **Key terms**
>
> Secondary hazard The indirect effects that result from the main (primary) impact of a hazard.
>
> Epicentre The point on the Earth's surface directly above the focus of an earthquake.

- at the moment of fracture rocks may regain their original shape but in a new position
- the depth of **focus** of an earthquake is significant:
  - □ shallow earthquakes (0–70 km) (75% of all energy released) cause the most damage
  - □ intermediate (70–300 km) and deep (300–700 km) earthquakes have much less effect

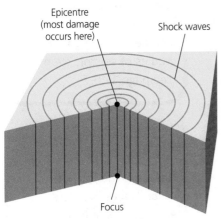

Figure 29 **The focus and epicentre of an earthquake**

# Waves and magnitude

Earthquakes generate three types of seismic (shock) wave:
- P-waves (primary waves) are the fastest — they arrive first, and cause the least damage
- S-waves (secondary waves) arrive next and shake the ground violently
- L-waves (Love waves) arrive last as they travel only across the surface — they have a large amplitude, a rolling movement and cause significant damage, including fracturing the ground

Magnitude:
- the energy release is measured by the logarithmic moment magnitude scale (MMS), a modification of the Richter scale
- damaging effects are measured by the Mercalli scale, which measures intensity of shaking

# Other effects

In the longer term, evidence for past earthquakes can be seen in:
- faulting in rocks — often visible on cliff faces
- inward-facing scarps in areas where a rift valley has been created

## Key terms

**Focus** The point below the Earth's surface where an earthquake occurs.

**Richter scale** The traditional measure of the energy release of an earthquake — superseded by the more accurate MMS, and now used only by the media.

## Exam tip

Note that these features are more likely to have originated from plate movements, where earthquakes would have taken place. They are more to do with association than cause.

# Hazards

## Impacts

Primary hazards:

■ ground-shaking and displacement, vertically and horizontally
■ damage depends on:
  □ depth of focus — decreases with depth
  □ distance from epicentre — decreases with distance
  □ local geology — more unconsolidated rocks are most damaged

Secondary hazards:

■ large landslides and avalanches — especially in mountainous areas such as Nepal and parts of China; landslides can block rivers and create large lakes, which when they overflow can be extremely dangerous
■ liquefaction — earthquakes compact the sediments where the ground consists of loose sediments of silts, sands and gravels that are waterlogged; they force the water to the surface, undermining buildings and roads

Tsunamis:

■ most tsunamis are generated by submarine earthquakes at subduction zones
■ the sea bed is displaced vertically (up or down)
■ this motion displaces a large volume of water in the ocean column, which then moves outwards from the point of displacement
■ when they are out at sea they have a very long wavelength, often in excess of 100 km
■ they are very short in amplitude, at around 1 m in height, and are barely noticeable
■ they travel very quickly, often at speeds of up to 700 km h$^{-1}$
■ when they reach land they rapidly increase in height, up to more than 25 m in some cases
■ they are often preceded by a localised drop in sea level (drawback) as water is drawn back and up by the approaching tsunami
■ they hit a coastline as a series of waves (a wave-train), more akin to a flood

### Exam tip

An earthquake's impact can be judged in terms of its primary and secondary effects, and the environmental, social, economic and political consequences, short and long term. Make sure you include these in your case studies of seismic events (see page 113).

### Exam tip

Research the impact of landslides in recent earthquakes in Nepal, and the damming of lakes in the Sichuan (China) earthquake (2008).

### Exam tip

Despite being commonly called 'tidal waves', tsunamis have nothing to do with tides.

### Synoptic link

Consider possible influences of your chosen physical landscape on the nature of seismic hazards.

### Do you know?

1 Why did the Tōhoku earthquake and subsequent tsunami have such a great impact on the world?
2 Can earthquakes be predicted?
3 What is a seismograph?

# 6.4 Living in hazard zones

## You need to know

- there is a range of impacts that people experience as a result of volcanic eruptions
- there is a range of impacts that people experience as a result of earthquake activity

# The impacts of living in a hazard zone

Whether people live in tectonically active locations depends on the level of **risk** they face in that area. This depends on:

- records of past events
- the time gap since the last event ('gap theory')
- the nature of the tectonic activity in the area
- attitudes to risk
- the level of **resilience** of the people who could be affected

## Key terms

**Risk** The probability of a hazard occurring and creating a loss of lives and/or livelihoods.

**Resilience** The degree to which a population or environment can absorb a hazardous event and yet remain within the same state of organisation, i.e. its ability to cope with stress and recover.

## Case study: Impacts of volcanoes

You are required to have case studies of **two** countries at contrasting levels of economic development.

Each case study must illustrate:

- reasons why people choose to live in tectonically active locations
- the impacts people experience as a result of **volcanic eruptions**
- the economic, environmental and political impacts on the country

## Exam tip

Possible examples include:
- **ACs** — Japan (Mount Fuji), Iceland (Eyjafjallajökull), Italy (Vesuvius, Etna), USA (Mt St Helens)
- **EDCs** — Indonesia (Merapi), Montserrat (La Soufrière)
- **LIDCs** — Cameroon (Nyiragongo)

## Case study: Impacts of earthquakes

You are required to have case studies of **two** countries at contrasting levels of economic development.

Each case study must illustrate:

- reasons why people choose to live in tectonically active locations
- the impacts people experience as a result of **earthquake activity**
- the economic, environmental and political impacts on the country

## Synoptic link

Consider the influence of 'character of place' when studying the impacts of a volcanic eruption.

# 6.5 Management

## Strategies to manage hazards

### Mitigating against the event

Table 41 shows methods used to mitigate against events.

Table 41 **Mitigating against the event**

| Nature of modification | Benefits | Issues |
|---|---|---|
| Land-use zoning:<br>- avoiding building on low-lying coasts (tsunamis)<br>- avoiding areas close to volcanoes<br>- avoiding areas where liquefaction is likely | - low cost<br>- relocates people from areas of high risk | - prevents economic development in some coastal areas<br>- requires strict enforcement |
| Tsunami defences:<br>- building sea walls and breakwaters | - reduces damage<br>- provides a sense of security | - can be overtopped<br>- very high cost<br>- unsightly |
| Lava diversion:<br>- channels<br>- water cooling | - diverts lava away from people and buildings<br>- relatively low cost | - works only for basaltic lava<br>- not feasible for majority of explosive volcanoes |

# Mitigating against vulnerability

Table 42 shows methods used to mitigate against vulnerability.

Table 42 **Mitigating against vulnerability**

| Nature of modification | Benefits | Issues |
|---|---|---|
| Hi-tech monitoring:<br>■ used to monitor volcanoes and predict eruptions | ■ prediction can be reasonably accurate<br>■ warnings/evacuation save lives | ■ costly — only found in developed/ emerging countries<br>■ possibility of **cry wolf syndrome**<br>■ property is still damaged |
| Community preparedness and education:<br>■ **earthquake kits**<br>■ preparation days<br>■ risk education | ■ low cost — can be organised by NGOs<br>■ can save lives at a local scale | ■ property is still damaged<br>■ harder to implement in isolated rural areas |
| Aseismic buildings:<br>■ cross-bracing<br>■ using counterweights<br>■ deep foundations | ■ protects people and property<br>■ financially possible in the developed world<br>■ basic design can be replicated in developing world | ■ high costs for tall buildings<br>■ older buildings and homes for people on low incomes are too difficult to protect |
| Adaptation:<br>■ moving out of danger areas and relocating | ■ saves lives and property | ■ difficult in densely populated areas<br>■ disrupts people's lives |

## Key terms

**Cry wolf syndrome** Occurs when predictions prove to be wrong, so that people are less likely to believe the next prediction and warning, and therefore fail to evacuate.

**Earthquake kits** Boxes of essential household supplies (water, food, battery-powered radio, blankets) kept in a safe place at home to be used in the days following an earthquake.`

# Mitigating against losses

Table 43 shows methods used to mitigate against losses.

Table 43 **Mitigating against losses**

| Nature of modification | Benefits | Issues |
|---|---|---|
| Emergency aid:<br>■ search and rescue followed by emergency food, water and shelter | ■ reduces death toll<br>■ keeps people alive until government help arrives | ■ costly — with difficulties reaching isolated areas<br>■ emergency services often limited and poorly equipped in EDCs and LIDCs |
| Long-term aid:<br>■ reconstruction<br>■ improvements to resilience | ■ incorporates land-use planning<br>■ establishes better construction methods | ■ very high cost<br>■ initial plans and ambitions not met in time |
| Insurance:<br>■ compensation given | ■ allows economic recovery | ■ does not save lives<br>■ few people in EDCs and LIDCs can afford insurance |

## Exam tip

Note that different types of mitigation are more applicable to some types of tectonic hazards than others.

## Synoptic link

Note that all forms of mitigation are dependent on the degree of governance within the area affected.

## Case study: Strategies to cope with volcanoes

You are required to have case studies of **two** countries at contrasting levels of economic development to illustrate strategies used to cope with **volcanic activity**.

Each case study must illustrate attempts to mitigate against:

- the event
- vulnerability
- losses

## Case study: Strategies to cope with earthquakes

You are required to have case studies of **two** countries at contrasting levels of economic development to illustrate strategies used to cope with **hazards from earthquakes**.

Each case study must illustrate attempts to mitigate against:

- the event
- vulnerability
- losses

### Exam tip

You can use the same case studies you used in Section 6.4 Living in hazard zones. Indeed, it makes sense to. Possible examples include:

- **ACs** — Japan (Mount Fuji), Iceland (Eyjafjallajökull), Italy (Vesuvius, Etna), USA (Mt St Helens)
- **EDCs** — Indonesia (Merapi), Montserrat (La Soufrière)
- **LIDCs** — Cameroon (Nyiragongo)

### Synoptic link

Consider the influence of 'character of place' when studying the management of a volcanic eruption.

### Synoptic link

Consider the influence of 'character of place' when studying the management of a seismic event.

### Exam tip

You can use the same case studies you used in Section 6.4 Living in hazard zones. Indeed, it makes sense to. Possible examples include:

- **ACs** — Japan (Kobe, Tōhoku), Italy (Amatrice and L'Aquila), New Zealand (Christchurch), USA (Northridge)
- **EDCs** — India (Gujarat), Mexico (Mexico City), Indonesia (Banda Aceh)
- **LIDCs** — Nepal (Ghorka), Haiti (Port-au-Prince)

# Variations over time

The risks from tectonic hazards change over time. The exposure to risk from volcanoes and earthquakes varies according to:

- their frequency and magnitude — in general, the lower the frequency, the greater the magnitude
- the nature of the secondary hazards created at the same time
- the number of people living in the area at the time

## The hazard risk equation

The hazard risk equation helps make clear the relationship between hazards and **disasters**:

$$\text{risk} = \text{hazard} \times \text{vulnerability/capacity to cope}$$

### Key terms

**Disaster** When a hazard exceeds the capacity of a country or area to cope with the effects of that hazard.

**Vulnerability** The risk of exposure to hazards combined with an inability to cope with them.

Some communities have a high resilience (see Tables 41–43). They can reduce the chances of disasters occurring by:

■ having emergency evacuation, rescue and relief systems in place
■ helping each other to reduce numbers affected
■ having hazard-resistant design or land-use planning to reduce the numbers at risk

# The Park model

The Park model illustrates:
■ how quality of life is impacted by a hazardous event
■ how a range of management strategies can be used over time — from before the event to after the event
■ the roles of emergency relief agencies and rehabilitation
■ that different areas affected may have a different response curve, depending on:
  □ physical factors — speed of onset, magnitude and duration
  □ human factors — quality of monitoring, level of preparedness and economic development, quality and quantity of relief mechanisms

## Synoptic link

Note the Park disaster response model contains elements of 'place', governance and global economic systems within it.

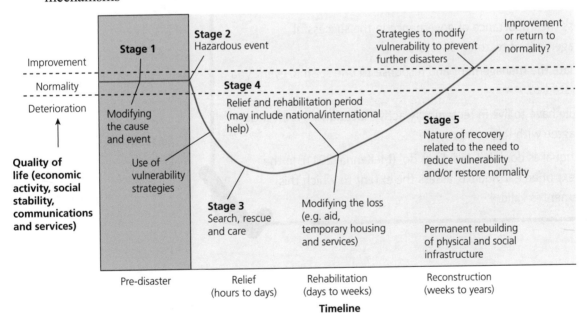

Figure 30 The Park disaster response model

## Exam tip

Be prepared to apply the Park model to each of the case studies you examine for volcanoes and earthquakes. Try to look for both similarities and differences in all of these events.

## Do you know?

1  Explain how the level of risk can change over time.
2  Explain how the speed of onset of a hazard can be critical.
3  What is aseismic design?
4  Why does it appear that there has been an increase in the number of disasters arising from tectonic hazards in recent years?

## End of section 6 questions

1  Describe the global distribution of volcanoes.
2  Explain the causes of tsunamis.
3  Explain the development of hazards found at convergent (destructive) plate margins.
4  With reference to examples, outline the ways in which the nature of volcanic hazards can vary.
5  Explain how fossil records can be used as evidence of continental drift and plate tectonics theory.
6  Examine how the risks from tectonic hazards affect placemaking processes.
7  Assess the importance of governance in the successful management of tectonic disasters.
8  Evaluate the management and response to one seismic event you have studied.
9  'People have to live in tectonically active locations.' How far do you agree with this statement?
10 'Earthquakes don't kill, buildings do' (McKenna, 2011). In the context of an earthquake, assess the extent to which this statement is valid.